PRAISE

"Millennials have been the subject of many a boardroom discussion and Costin's book is a go-to guide for every company looking to serve this highly relevant but often misunderstood market segment."

SANGEET PAUL CHOUDARY
best-selling co-author of *Platform Revolution,* which was
an HBR Top 10 must-read in 2017

"If you're a member of Gen X or the Baby Boomer generation and you find yourself mystified by Millennials (or worse—waging class warfare with them), yet, they are your customers, this book will open your eyes. You'll understand what they want, and most importantly, *why they want it.* Firms who ignore Gui's advice will be out of business by 2025. The clock is ticking."

PERRY MARSHALL
author of *Ultimate Guide to Facebook
Advertising* and *80/20 Sales & Marketing*

"Gui has insightfully hit on one of the biggest challenges that organizations face today: how to successfully connect with and influence the next generation of consumers. Everyone should be thinking about the future and how to adapt and evolve to the new way of doing business. His step-by-step approach to embrace and learn from the changing market dynamics holds true for organizations—regardless of size or industry—that want to succeed in engaging with the Millennial generation and beyond."

WILL FULLER
EVP, Lincoln Financial Group

"After reading this book, Millennials will no longer be what I believe is the 'most-misunderstood generation.' Gui Costin brings powerful insight to the how and why Millennials will actually go down in history as the 'impact generation.'"

DAVID NOVAK
former chairman of YUM Brands and #1 best-selling
author of *Taking People With You*

MILLENNIALS ARE NOT ALIENS

MILLENNIALS

ARE NOT

ALIENS

...but they are
80 Million Americans
Who Are Changing How We Buy, Sell,
Vacation, Invest, and **Just About Everything Else**

GUI COSTIN

ForbesBooks

Published by ForbesBooks, Charleston, South Carolina.
Member of Advantage Media Group.

ForbesBooks is a registered trademark, and the ForbesBooks colophon is a trademark of Forbes Media, LLC.

Printed in the United States of America.

10 9 8 7 6 5 4 3 2 1

ISBN: 978-1-946633-42-2
LCCN: 2018966658

Cover design by George Stevens.
Layout design by Melanie Cloth.

This publication is designed to provide accurate and authoritative information in regard to the subject matter covered. It is sold with the understanding that the publisher is not engaged in rendering legal, accounting, or other professional services. If legal advice or other expert assistance is required, the services of a competent professional person should be sought.

Advantage Media Group is proud to be a part of the Tree Neutral® program. Tree Neutral offsets the number of trees consumed in the production and printing of this book by taking proactive steps such as planting trees in direct proportion to the number of trees used to print books. To learn more about Tree Neutral, please visit **www.treeneutral.com**.

Since 1917, the Forbes mission has remained constant. Global Champions of Entrepreneurial Capitalism. ForbesBooks exists to further that aim by bringing the Stories, Passion, and Knowledge of top thought leaders to the forefront. ForbesBooks brings you The Best in Business. To be considered for publication, please visit **www.forbesbooks.com**.

This book is dedicated to Alan Breed, the team at Edgewood Management, and Lenny Ward. Had Lenny not introduced me to Alan and had Edgewood not hired me, nothing in my career would have been possible. I owe it all to them. Thank you.

TABLE OF CONTENTS

PART ONE

PART TWO

ACKNOWLEDGMENTS

I would like to thank Salina Jivani and Perry O'Grady who helped me write and edit the book. Without them, this book would have never gotten off the ground. I would also like to thank the entire team at Advantage|ForbesBooks for helping me make the idea of this book a reality. Lastly, I'd like to thank Bill Davis of Stance Capital for writing Chapter 9 on Impact Investing and Millennials, where he so articulately brings the Millennial mindset to life.

INTRODUCTION

This book got its start in a conference room outside of Philadelphia in 2015. That summer, I was leading a sales team meeting at the firm I manage during which one of our salespeople began bemoaning the fact that he was having a tough time getting clients to meet with him. The people he thought he knew had changed and the way things were done had changed along with them. Prospects were outright telling him that although they liked his proposed investment strategy, they simply did not have the time to meet with him—or the time to underwrite or give due diligence to his strategy.

Our firm, Dakota Holdings, is an eleven-person sales and marketing business for boutique investment firms. Managers hire us to raise money for their investment strategies. Since our inception, we have raised over $20 billion for fifteen different investment strategies.

While I was not surprised by the time aspect of the salesperson's story, I was surprised by the "even though I like it" part. If the buyer tells you he or she likes your product but cannot take action because of the time it takes to underwrite it, then you have a big problem. For me, this statement was an epiphany. I knew right then that the game had changed. If we were going to score wins going forward, we had to make it easier for due diligence analysts by doing more of the heavy lifting for them.

At Dakota, we have always prided ourselves in doing as much of the work as possible for the buyer; this facilitates the process and leads to more successful sales. Anyone who markets institutional investment strategies for a living knows how time consuming it is for an analyst to fully give due diligence to a strategy. The salesperson's story clarified the fact that we could no longer rely on our prospects to make the time to fully embrace a strategy. They were simply too busy.

At the same time, I was seeing for myself and hearing from the team that most of the people we were meeting with were under age forty. The buyers we once knew had morphed into Millennials. I knew that Millennial buying behaviors were different, but I did not know quite how much.

So here we were, facing a new challenge: buyers who had no time, buyers who were now under age forty, and buyers whose buying behaviors we knew next to nothing about. One thing was clear about these new-age buyers, however: They did not like meeting with people if they could avoid it. The question then became: how do we create a situation where we can make the buying process more efficient while at the same time appealing to this new buying behavior?

It was clear to me that the investment business was already hurtling down the same digital content path that many other industries had already traveled. The future holds a world where due diligence analysts will be able to easily search for and find free, high-quality due diligence level content on any investment strategy without having to first speak to someone.

I wrote this book to capture what we have learned and how we, as a firm, have pivoted to meet the needs of the primary buyer in our business: the Millennial. Millennials buy differently than previous generations, which means Gen Xers and Baby Boomers are having to adjust their sales and marketing strategies.

But why this focus on Millennials when there are still others in the market? The Millennial generation is the largest segment of the population, comprising approximately 80 million people in the United States and 2.5 billion globally. They are currently the dominating segment of the workforce.

After my epiphany, I got my hands on every piece of research I could find on Millennial behaviors and how to effectively reach them. I have read a lot and supplemented this knowledge by speaking directly to the authors and researchers. The bulk of my learning has come from four books: *Exponential Organizations* by Salim Ismail and Michael Malone; *Platform Scale* by Sangeet Paul Choudary; *Platform Revolution* by Sangeet Paul Choudary, Geoffrey Parker, and Marshall Van Alstyne; and *Modern Monopolies* by Alex Moazed and Nicholas Johnson. All of these books make it clear that platforms are going to dominate the world, as we are seeing from firms like Facebook, Amazon, PayPal, LinkedIn, Instagram, Google, YouTube, and Twitter.

> CHANGE, GROWTH, AND EVOLUTION ARE CLEARLY THE NEW NORMS.

Although our direct sales effort and approach has not changed since 2015, we have significantly enhanced our activities to adopt methods we previously never explored. Today, we shoot videos, host podcasts, analyze user engagement, track downloads, create surveys, populate YouTube channels, and post to LinkedIn, Facebook, and Twitter.

The book is a shortcut for you. I have distilled all of the work and research we have done into the contents of this book to help you move forward more quickly and gain better insight into the Millennial generation and how it differs from previous ones. We will compare and contrast Millennials, Gen Xers, and Baby Boomers, discuss the Content Economy, explore video and its importance, talk about mindset and adapting, and share tips and techniques for adjusting to the Millennial mindset.

For those who are looking to get a general idea of the changes happening around us, Part 1 of this book is for you. Here, I will walk you through what is happening to the landscape around us as well as give you a peek into the investment industry at a macro-level. This is largely where we will talk about the changes in consumer behaviors and how that is impacting and will continue to impact us as a society.

If you are in the investment industry, read Part 1, but also make sure to carry on to Part 2—this is where I focus more directly on the investment space and how the transformation in buyers and their purchasing behaviors affects boutique investment firms. Here, I discuss the effects Millennials are having on wealth management, investment management, and impact investing.

I hope you enjoy the read and gain plenty of insight and information along the way to help you in your current or future endeavors.

Best wishes,

Gui

PART ONE

CHAPT

TER 1

HERE COMES
TECHNOLOGY—
AND THE
MILLENNIALS

"Hello. XYZ Books. How may I help you?"

"Yes, I'm calling to see if you have the new Steve Jobs book in stock?"

Sure, hold one moment and let me go check the shelf."

Five minutes later. "No, I'm sorry. We do not have it in stock, but we can order it for you."

"Maybe. Can I see if you have the other Steve Jobs book in stock. I think the title is like Simple or Simplicity."

Typing.

"It says we have it in stock—let me check."

Another five minutes later. "Thanks for holding. Yes, we have it. Would you like me to put it aside?"

"That would be great. I'll drive over and pick it up this evening."

That was life before the Internet. Baby Boomers are used to brick and mortar and telephones—and these concepts are not completely alien to Gen Xers, either. But the Internet, Amazon, and Google have changed the way we buy.

If you want to purchase a book today, it can be delivered to you tomorrow from a number of outlets. You don't even have to leave your home. A salesclerk might as well be a blacksmith or telegraph operator—no one needs them anymore.

You already know this. So why are we talking about it and what does it even have to do with what we're examining?

To understand that, you should first know this: we are living in a Content Economy. Very briefly, the Content Economy is an economy in which consumers—mainly Millennials—are becoming more and more dependent on quality, digital content to make buying decisions. This means we're more reliant on the web than we are on a salesclerk. Later, we will talk in greater detail about the Content Economy.

But what this example demonstrates is that buying habits are changing. It proves that no matter how successful certain tactics were in the past, they are not the way things are done anymore. Thanks to technology and the Content Economy, we do not call bookstores anymore, we simply push a few buttons to see what is in stock and to purchase an item.

We will talk more about the Content Economy and what it is in Chapter 3. For now, the main point to absorb is that change happens fast and there is no indication that it is slowing down, thanks to technology. As we all know, technology has transformed what we do, how we do it, and how fast we do it. It has also transformed our expectations.

All of us, regardless of which generation we belong to, have been impacted by technology. My dad is seventy-five years old and loves Amazon. But the generation most affected by the digital, connected world are the Millennials.

You could think of it this way: If technology were a geyser, Baby Boomers and Generation Xers have been sprayed by its impact, but Millennials got drenched. So while technology's pull is most evident in Millennials, that does not mean everyone else escaped it.

Technology and the Internet have single-handedly influenced the way people buy, and its largest users are Millennials. In other words, technology impacts buying behaviors of all people, but its heaviest users are Millennials.

There is a reason I am stressing this point. It is because we are about to focus on the Millennial consumer. As we discuss their attributes, it is easy to be misled into believing that they are responsible for the Content Economy, or for the evolution in the way we consume content or for the shift of the tectonic plates beneath our feet in the investment industry.

I hear it all the time. "It's because of the Millennials that we have to do this," or "It's because of them that we have to change that." People think it is the Millennials who emerged and influenced society and shook things up. But it is really the tools they were handed that created the change.

It is not a specific population that is responsible for the changes we have seen in the past decade or so, but rather the technology— often created by Baby Boomers or Gen Xers—that enabled so many of those changes. The timing of the changes meant that Millennials, as the largest consumers of that technology, happen to be the conduit of that change. As such, they unfortunately bear the brunt of much of the largely undue criticism of why and how things have changed.

The Internet disrupted patterns of behavior relied on by generations, which are foreign to Millennials. Many Millennials never used the Yellow Pages, an Encyclopedia, a rotary dial phone. They never called a store to check an item's availability, browsed the aisles of a video rental store, or felt excited about speaking to a salesperson.

Because technology is such an important part of Millennials' DNA, we need to tackle the relationship between Millennials and technology first. Once we do that, you will be able to make better sense of how they behave and see the world.

ON THE CUTTING EDGE OF TECHNOLOGY

As we have established, Baby Boomers were molded by an environment in which telephones and brick and mortar dominated. In contrast, Gen Xers were raised amid bursts of innovation and technology.

For Millennials, the biggest influencer is technology. Most were in their early-to-late teenage years when the likes of Ask Jeeves and MySpace became available, which of course gave way to titans like Google and Facebook. Facebook paved the way for an onslaught of social media platforms, such as Pinterest, Instagram, Twitter, and Tumblr, to name just a few.

> ## EVEN THE WAY MILLENNIALS WERE SCHOOLED WAS DIFFERENT, THANKS TO TECHNOLOGY.

For example, when I went to school, we used microfiche to do research. Microfiche was a piece of film that contained pictures of old newspaper, magazine, or catalogue clippings. To view the images, you had to insert the film under a microfiche reader, which would magnify the clippings. A "search" meant reading the text. That was how you would get credible source material for research papers and projects.

Search engines and the Internet changed the world for Millennials. It turned them into self-educators, allowing them to learn without formal instruction, which is why I dub them the Self-Education Generation. Schools raced to keep up with the Internet, creating technology labs with rows and rows of desktop computers to encourage students to learn basic concepts like browsing the web for research projects.

Not only did technology begin to intertwine with Millennials' lives at school, but it also became a crucial centerpiece at home, where Millennials spent hours on newfound applications like instant messengers and email, thanks to the advent of web portals like Netscape and AOL. And then the smartphone came along and changed everything.

Now, we have Siri in our back pockets and Alexa in our homes.

If you are a Baby Boomer or Gen Xer, would you ever have imagined that one day you would be able to stand inside your house, open the blinds, peer outside, and say, "Hey Alexa, what is the weather going to be like?" More importantly, would you have understood the value of asking about the weather while actually looking at the weather?

Twenty years ago, if I told you you would one day come to rely on someone named Alexa, you would probably wonder who in the world Alexa is and what significance she would bear in your life. You would never have guessed she would be the Amazon version of Rosie from the Jetsons.

In fact, just the other day I was standing in my kitchen, rifling through my medicine cabinet when I noticed I was almost out of fish oil pills. Without thinking, I turned over my shoulder and said, "Alexa, order fish oil pills." And, boom—it was done.

I have adapted to technology as a Gen Xer, even though it came into my life much later.

This is the world Millennials know. Alexa is just another tool at their disposal. As soon as a thought or question pops into their minds, they have the luxury of instant gratification—an instantaneous answer at their fingertips. It is what they have grown up with from an early age. Technology like Alexa is not a far-fetched idea; inventions like these are de rigueur.

I hear people say it all the time: Millennials are different. They do things differently. They have a different mindset. And it is true.

Think about why. It is the "why" that matters for a discussion of the Content Economy.

Technology and the Internet has shaped Millennials' life, personalities, perceptions, mindset, habits, the way they consume content, and the way they buy. Remember, Millennials are not the creators of the Content Economy, but they are the underpinning of the Content Economy because they embraced its possibilities.

With that context, let's learn more about who the Millennials actually are.

EVERYTHING YOU NEED TO KNOW ABOUT MILLENNIALS

Tom Brokaw, the former NBC News anchor, calls Millennials the "greatest generation since the 'Greatest Generation.'" Perhaps that is because they have surpassed the population of Baby Boomers, which makes sense since they have been borne out of the Boomer generation. Perhaps it is because they are distinctive from preceding generations thanks to their mastery and adoption of a multitude of technologies. Whatever the reason, this segment of the population, born roughly between 1981 and 1995, is now in the driver's seat of the global workforce.

Personally, I believe Millennials are the most important generation because of their sheer size and ability or desire to share information rapidly.

Bargaining is a part of their process. Most Millennials see a price tag as superfluous, not something that dictates the actual price of a product but rather a number they should aim to beat to secure the best bargain. Because they are facile with technology, they rely heavily on their cell phones to price shop and hunt the best deals.[1]

---

1   SEO.com, "Video Marketing to Millennials," https://www.seo.com/blog/video-marketing-to-millennials.

Buying is sharing. For Millennials, making a purchase is an event to be shared with their social media network. A new car? A fancy pair of shoes? A dinner at an elite restaurant? Scroll through a Millennial's social media "feed" and you will probably see a barrage of images revealing the day's purchases. With so many of them sharing their buys to friends and strangers, a kind of competition develops.

It is also not uncommon for Millennials to candidly share details about their buying experiences post-purchase, good or bad, on their public social media platforms. This can translate to bad news for businesses that underperform or, conversely, great news for those that exceed expectations. Sites like Yelp have created platforms to monetize this type of feedback.

Big purchases can happen virtually. Would you ever conceive of buying a car without ever physically seeing or touching it first? Millennials do it all the time. In fact, they are the very first of all the generations to make a large purchase without first performing an on-site inspection.

Brand loyalty means something. No matter how fickle many believe Millennials to be, they are, in fact, extremely brand loyal. In fact, 60 percent of Millennials say they almost always stick to brands they currently purchase.[2]

Smartphones are a necessity. Smartphones are important to everyone, but they are particularly important to Millennials who use them for every aspect of their lives. According to SDL, Millennials touch their smartphones forty-three times a day, relying on them for

---

2   Zofia Antonow, "The millennial consumer: how they shop & why they buy," Ascend, February 28, 2018, https://www.agencyascend.com/blog/millennial-consumer-how-they-shop-why-they-buy.

everything from email to social media to organization and planning, among an endless list of other tasks.[3]

> **Smartphones are a necessity. Smart-phones are important to everyone, but they are particularly important to Millennials who use them for every aspect of their lives.**

Information is essential. More often than not, you will catch a Millennial scouring information on the web before making a purchase to learn about a brand or product. The breadth of their research includes poring through websites, blogs, or peer reviews they trust. Based on interviews with Jason Dorsey, an acclaimed expert speaker and researcher on the topic of Millennials, many even admit that reviews can make or break their decision to make a serious purchase.

Instant gratification is paramount. Because they have grown up in a digital age, Millennials are used to speed and immediate gratification—the dopamine response. They value prompt feedback and communication and do not like wasting time; think emails, text messages, and online messaging. Because they have grown so accustomed to speed, Millennials rely on these applications beyond just personal use, which is why you will find many of these applications as embedded channels of communication in many workplace environments.

---

3   "SDL Study Reveals Channels Are Irrelevant to Consumers," SDL, July 14, 2014, https://www.sdl.com/about/news-media/press/2014/sdl-study-reveals-channels-are-irrelevant-to-consumers.html.

Technology is important at work. As we have established, this generation is heavily dependent on technology for pretty much every aspect of their lives, from making purchases to keeping in touch with friends and even dating. Technology has converged with their daily existence to the point that this generation no longer requests for it to be present in their workplace, they expect it.

People sometimes mistake these expectations to mean that Millennials act entitled to special privilege, but what a Baby Boomer or Gen Xer might consider a privilege is actually just a routine part of life for Millennials.

What many fail to understand is that because technology is woven into the fiber of their very beings, Millennials cannot imagine life without it. It is what they know. A recent study done by LivePerson asked Milennials how much money someone would have to pay them for them to relinquish their smartphones for the rest of their lives. A staggering 43 percent said $5 million or more.[4] My son said $100 million. It is what they are used to using. And they believe that by having these technologies present in their workplace, they will be more efficient at their jobs.

Following the post-World War II migration to the suburbs, much of America became dependent on cars. If I told you to ride to work in a horse and carriage, not only would you look at me like I was nuts, but you would not know the first thing about how to operate one. Once you know how to drive a car, that is what you know and there is no going back to the ways of the past.

In the same way, Millennials are used to technology. They are not used to manual processes. They are used to digital not paper. Do you

---

4   Matt Hopkins, "Here's One For Ya: Would You Totally Ditch Your Smartphone For $5 Million?" Pedestrian, October 18, 2017, https://www.pedestrian.tv/money/give-up-smartphones-5-mil.

think they'd print out directions for a road trip? For them to expect technology to transcend through from their personal to their professional lives is, in their mind, a natural transition and expectation.

The environment within which you grow up determines to what you become accustomed. That is why I am writing this book—to shake up all you Gen Xers and Baby Boomers so you realize that how you grew up is affecting the way you are selling and marketing your organizations. You cannot sell and market to Millennials the same way you were sold and marketed to.

The good news is, many companies are listening. They are actively replacing dated, manual processes with more efficient, cutting-edge tools to promote the convenience and speed Millennials crave.

Motivation is within them. Older generations have labeled Millennials as lazy and inefficient. Contrary to that perception, Millennials do have tremendous drive. Give them a chance to improve their personal and professional environment and you might be surprised at how ambitiously and diligently they will work toward that goal.

Although notoriously labeled the "job-hopping" generation, Millennials are loyal to companies who invest and take an interest in their professional and personal growth. In fact, according to a 2016 Gallup poll, an astounding 87 percent of Millennials said that professional development was important to them, making their desire to learn and flourish a key factor that distinguishes them from previous generations.[5]

That is why today, more than ever, learning management systems, training opportunities, and certification offerings are integral to attracting and retaining top Millennial talent.

---

5   Amy Adkins and Brandon Rigoni, "Millennials Want Jobs to Be Development Opportunities," Gallup, June 30, 2016, https://news.gallup.com/businessjournal/193274/millennials-jobs-development-opportunities.aspx.

Millennials are also ambitious when it comes to taking action for things that they feel impassioned about. For example, 41 percent claim to have taken an active role in an initiative, such as protesting at a march or promoting a campaign, whereas only 17 percent of Baby Boomers state the same.[6]

Millennials believe in setting their own timelines. More so than any previous generation, they have put off important milestones like buying homes, dating seriously, getting married, and having children. That is because Millennials have a completely different outlook on these key life milestones than any prior generation. A 2016 study found that while 21 percent of Millennials are married today, 48 percent of Baby Boomers were married at the same age.[7]

Many blame Millennials' apprehensions about progressing toward these familiar milestones at the same rate as previous generations on the Great Recession of 2008, their unprecedented level of education debt, and their fears about being able to find a stable, well-paying job.

Traditions are still valued. While technology is a key to the lives of Millennials, this generation also appreciates more traditional experiences, like dining at restaurants and seeing a movie in a theater. As evidence, *Forbes* provided an analysis of holiday spending during the 2016 holiday season. Millennials spent an average of $220, far surpassing the spending of Baby Boomers and Generation X.[8]

---

6   Sebastian Buck, "As Millennials Demand More Meaning, Older Brands Are Not Aging Well," Fast Company, October 5, 2017, https://www.fastcompany.com/40477211/ as-millennials-demand-more-meaning-older-brands-are-not-aging-well.

7   John Fleming, "Gallup Analysis: Millennials, Marriage and Family," Gallup, May 19, 2016, https://news.gallup.com/poll/191462/gallup-analysis-millennials-marriage-family.aspx.

8   Tom McGee, "How Millennials Are Changing Retail Patterns," Forbes, January 23, 2017,https://www.forbes.com/sites/tommcgee/2017/01/23/the-rise-of-the-millennial/#7ca670fd5f74.

They are a self-education and self-service generation. While I acknowledge that much of the evidence is anecdotal, I have worked extensively with buyers and due diligence analysts, the majority of whom are Millennials. My experience is that they appreciate being self-taught and being able to service themselves independently of outside help.

Millennials consume content to serve their needs. They do research. They browse sites. If they want to learn a new skill, they learn it independently, often without an instructor or professional schooling. With Google, YouTube, blogs, Pinterest, and Yelp at Millennials' disposal, it empowers them in their desire to tackle things themselves. They are able to freely explore and learn anything and everything as they wish. So that is exactly what they do.

To help us understand how these traits are put into play, let us take a look at the workday of a typical Millennial.

A DAY IN THE LIFE OF A WORKING MILLENNIAL

It is 2018. Jacob wakes up to his cell phone cooing a customized tune that he downloaded from an app he found in the app store.

He spends the first fifteen minutes of his day checking his cell phone for texts, calls, social media alerts, and emails. He showers, gets dressed, and calls an Uber that drops him off at the coffee shop just down the street from his office. He grabs a latte and protein breakfast bar to keep himself satisfied until lunch.

Jacob's office has an open-plan collaborative workspace, which means he has almost no privacy. He pulls his laptop out of his backpack, pushes it into the docking station, and is ready for work.

When he has a question about an upcoming deadline, he "Slacks" his boss and receives an immediate response. At noon, Jacob calls Uber Eats, which delivers his lunch in less than twenty minutes.

The worst part of his day is when the office Internet crashes. He decides to leave work early and work a few hours remotely from home. Just as he is putting away his dinner dishes, the garbage disposal makes a funny sound, the drain gets clogged, and the switch will not work. Jacob whips out his cell phone, finds a tutorial on YouTube, and in under ten minutes, he has figured out how to fix the disposal.

Jacob finishes his day falling asleep while playing a video game on his cell phone.

Notice that Jacob has a slew of technologies at his fingertips, the most critical one being his cell phone.

Technology is at his beck and call at all times, making daily tasks like getting to work, connecting with colleagues, ordering lunch, and fixing things that he would otherwise have no knowledge about part of his daily routine.

WHY IT ALL MATTERS

The examples illustrate what you need to know, in the context of this book, about technology and how it is defining Millennials.

Hopefully you also realize how technology has changed nearly every aspect of how we do things today, from working to buying to learning to interacting with others.

You should also see how technology, with Millennials as its primary conduit, has sparked the rise of the Content Economy—an economy in which buying behaviors are influenced most by digital content. You should recognize how this digital content has empowered Millennials to be a self-service, self-education generation. If you are in the investment business, you know that we are nowhere close to providing for this self-service, self-education approach.

If you are a business owner outside of the boutique investment space, you are probably wondering why Millennials are so critically important given that there are other generations from whom you could be soliciting business. If that is a question running through your mind, let me present this fact: Millennials are forecast to control $24 trillion of the world's wealth by 2020.[9]

If you see yourself in business in 2020 or beyond, you will need to cater to Millennials. In fact, any brand or company will need to start shifting its focus in that direction, if they have not already, to avoid a downward spiral, or their business's ultimate demise.

Now that you have a clear understanding of who Millennials are, in the next chapter, we will explore the other two generations in the marketplace mix right now: Gen Xers and Baby Boomers. When we do, you will see the chasm, the rift, and the differences between these generations. And you will see that these differences must be bridged to create a successful collaboration between these three generations.

Key Takeaways

☑ Technology and the Internet has enabled the rise of the Content Economy by making content instantly available in many forms, including videos, websites, reviews, blog posts, and more.

---

9   Thomas Franck, "UBS reports millennials could be worth up to $24 trillion by 2020," CNBC, June 23, 2017, https://www.cnbc.com/2017/06/23/ubs-millennials-worth-24-trillion-by-2020.html.

- ☑ Millennials use technology and the content available through technology to make buying decisions.

- ☑ Millennials have seen a very rapid progression of technology from a young age.

- ☑ Technology dominates nearly every aspect of Millennials' lives.

- ☑ If you see your business growing, you must adapt to the buying behaviors of the Content Economy and to Millennials' habits and preferences.

CHAP

TER 2

THE REIGN OF GENERATION XERS AND BABY BOOMERS

Remember when you once drove without a smartphone clinging to your dashboard or without Siri commanding your every turn in her tinny, robotic drone?

Do you recall when payphones, classified ads, the Yellow Pages, White Pages, and encyclopedias were relevant, important resources?

It seems like ancient history, but it has only been only a few decades since our world transformed from a place in which the news was curated by someone behind the curtain and forced on us to a digital one delivered to us based on our interests through an accompaniment of beeps, buzzes, and chirps.

If you are familiar with this evolution, you are probably a Baby Boomer or a Generation Xer.

I remember those days. I remember what it was like growing up as a kid who watched shows on one of three main channels: CBS, ABC, NBC. Life is very different for my own kids, who happen to be Gen Zs, who even though are not the main topic of this book, also have very different consumption habits than their parents, but very similar to Millennials.

You will notice we discuss people in generational groups throughout this book. That is because an individual's generation matters. Each generation has its own reality, because, as we stated in the previous chapter, each is raised in different environments that affect its habits, tendencies, and mindsets. Environmental components during our lifetime shape the way we communicate, the way we perceive, and the way we think. They shape the way we conduct business. And they shape how businesses make modifications to interact with us as a segment of consumers and a target market.

Interestingly, in my industry, the investment business, there is a striking contrast between the people who run these firms today (i.e., forty-five- to seventy-five-year-old Boomers and Gen Xers) and the professional buyers (i.e., Millennials under forty). The investment business has "self-service content" in the form of quantitative content, but zero, and I mean zero, self-service qualitative content to learn anything about an investment strategy without having to talk to someone.

> **Environmental components during our lifetime shape the way we communicate, the way we perceive, and the way we think. They shape the way we conduct business. And they shape how businesses make modifications to interact with us as a segment of consumers and a target market.**

The investment business is stuck in the existing way of selling: send an email with PDF attachments, set-up a call or a meeting, and have the buyers—generally a Millennial—build their research from scratch. It's truly contrary to how the entire world works today and, ironically, how the best investors invest. The best investors have been investing in stocks of companies that are leaders in creating networks, content, communication tools, video, audio, payment systems, but in their own world they are stuck in 1995. No one can learn anything about them without talking to them.

To prevent you from learning the hard way on your own, I am hoping to spare you the pain and help you realize what is happening around us.

THE BLOOM OF THE BOOMERS

As World War II was ending in 1945, the men who served began returning home and the country was anxiously awaiting their return, none more so than their wives and sweethearts. And with their return came a boom: a big boom of babies.

This boom continued from approximately 1946 to 1964, accounting for nearly 77 million births in the United States alone. And this generation came to be known as the Baby Boomers.

With the halo of a great victory in war and the subsequent peace, life for Baby Boomers was pleasant. People yearned for a peaceful, stable life, opting to raise their growing families in quiet suburbs where homes were cheaper and a family could enjoy the trappings of success. Perhaps because of the shared experience of the war, people felt connected. If a neighbor was ill or needed help, they could reach out to a neighbor for aid.

People of the era grew up writing letters, practicing the art of penmanship, making phone calls, playing outdoors, and building great socializing and interpersonal skills. Many of their interactions were face-to-face, because that was the way to meet with people.

The defining characteristic of Baby Boomers is that they are hard workers, often prioritizing work before play. As a result, many of them pushed careers ahead of family life. They were also the architects of the "American Dream," of having kids, working a stable job, owning a home, and building a pension.

It was not until much later in their lives that personal communication technology took over. While this generation does use technology, it turns to it more for productivity and less for connectivity.

To this day, you are not likely to see Baby Boomers opt for text or email when there is a functioning phone within reach. Talking is what they are accustomed to doing. Baby Boomers may no longer be the largest generation, but they are still one of the biggest segments of the population, comprising almost 20 percent of US inhabitants alone. They are still an impactful segment.

In the previous chapter, we saw how Jacob, a Millennial, went about his day. Now let's rewind several decades to when his grandfather, James, was in the workforce full time. See if you can spot the major differences.

A DAY IN THE LIFE OF A WORKING BABY BOOMER

It's 1986 and James Michael is just starting his day to a blaring alarm clock. After taking a quick shower and changing into his suit and tie, he sits down at the table and enjoys a hearty breakfast of toast, eggs, and bacon with a glass of orange juice. Simultaneously, he browses through the newspaper.

After the most stressful part of his day—battling rush hour traffic—he settles into his cubicle at Gengis Corporation, where his view of the office has not changed in the past twenty years.

At noon, he enjoys a meal at the office cafeteria with his usual crew, paying for his lunch with cash. Sometime after lunch, he regards his ever-reliable watch (he has a whole collection) and heads to the conference room for the office afternoon meeting.

After the meeting, James realizes he has some outstanding questions about a project he is working on with a coworker, so he makes his way over to the coworker's cube to trade office gossip and get some answers.

Because he has an important presentation the next morning, he stays at work till nine.

Once he is finally home, James eats dinner by himself at the table with his favorite record playing on the record player. He puts the dishes away and notices the kitchen sink is clogged. It is too late to call a plumber, so he jots a note to himself on the notepad in his shirt pocket to call someone first thing in the morning.

When he is finally in bed, he pulls out an Agatha Christie favorite from the drawer of his side table and reads until he falls asleep.

Now let's meet James's successors, Generation X, to see how their lives differ.

GENERATION X

Generation X starts right at Baby Boomers' heels, covering approximately 1965-1980 and comprising approximately 45 million Americans. Often termed the "Lost Generation," Gen Xers are also known as the sandwich generation because they are the lesser-known group wedged between the popular Baby Boomers and Millennials.

Most Gen Xers grew up in dual- or single-parent Baby Boomer working households. As a result, they were the first generation to be scuttled off to daycare, earning them yet another designation as the "daycare generation."

Gen Xers are most popularly known as the "latchkey generation" for the lack of parental supervision and attention they were given as kids.

Growing up a Gen Xer was difficult in part because this generation was raised by parents who focused more on work than family. There is a general acknowledgement that this generation suffered from more distant parental relationships and more broken homes. As a result, kids of this generation were left to their own devices as they struggled to make sense of life and establish their identities.

Perhaps most significantly, Gen Xers were the first generation to grow up with personal computers, so they tend to be more flexible with their adaptation of technology than Baby Boomers.

Many Gen Xers saw their Baby Boomer parents, despite their diligence at work and lifelong loyalty to the same company, lose their jobs. Experiencing this loss firsthand is said to have influenced Gen Xers' own views on company loyalty, sparking their lack of commitment to working for a single organization in the way their parents had. Many of them have switched companies several times in their careers, making them more adept at embracing different company cultures. There is an argument that forced independence and greater job mobility influenced Gen Xers' ability to better adapt to life changes in general.

Perhaps because of the lack of attention they received from their own parents, many Gen Xers place a huge importance on being able to maintain a work-life balance between their careers and families.

To see the differences between Gen Xers and Baby Boomers, let's take a look at a story about Lindsay, James's daughter, who is a Generation Xer.

A DAY IN THE LIFE OF A WORKING GENERATION XER

It's 1995. Lindsay's day starts with her alarm clock blaring a Whitney Houston classic. After a quick shower and change, she enjoys a yogurt bowl and heads out to her car, buckling her seatbelt and pushing the lock down securely on the driver's side door. Midway through her commute, she encounters construction. The detour suggested by the construction signs gets her lost, so she pulls over, fishes a map from her glove compartment, and eventually finds her way to the office.

At work, as she is waiting for her desktop computer to boot up, she realizes she is bored with her job and ready for a change in career. After all, she has been with the company for two years and it is time to grow and move on to greener pastures.

During the morning, Lindsay has several questions about a project she is working on with a coworker, so she picks up the phone and calls him for answers.

When it is finally lunch time, her stomach is growling. Her pager buzzes, displaying the phone number of her friend Susan. Lindsay calls Susan and they decide to meet at a local eatery for lunch where Lindsay pays for her sandwich with her Visa credit card.

That night, she soaks in a nice warm bath to unwind while she plays the "Bath Mix" tape she made in her new dual-purpose CD/cassette player. Friday nights are her favorite because she gets to watch Steve Urkle (a leading character in the show *Family Matters*) and *Step-by-Step*, another popular show on cable, along with a whole marathon of her favorite weekly shows on ABC. She falls asleep with the television left on.

You can see some of the differences between Lindsay's generation and her father's. There is more technology: The CD/cassette player has replaced the record player. The credit card makes having cash less important. The phone supplants the walk around the office every time there is a question. The pager enables speedier communication. Television offers a broader selection of entertainment.

To sum it up, we are looking at two vastly different individuals who grew up during different eras.

Baby Boomers, generally:

- Are confident

- Are hardworking and career-driven and less family-oriented

- Value strong interpersonal communication skills

- Believe in company loyalty and commitment

- Are comfortable with manual processes

- Experienced limited change at their peak (compared to the subsequent generations)

Generation Xers, generally:

- Are not as rigid on the concept of company loyalty

- Are more adaptive to technology because they did see a few innovations during their prime (i.e. pagers)

- Are open to change as a result of working within several different company cultures

WHY GENERATION MATTERS

As it relates to this book, when you were born and the habits that you developed at that time due to technological developments are significant because changing habits is difficult. The habits that Baby Boomers had to adapt to for Gen Xers was less radical than what we are going through currently. The way things are done today is almost unrecognizable from the 60s, 70s, 80s, and 90s.

The generation of your birthdate shapes your way of doing things, largely based on the tools available at the time.

In the same way that farming evolved man from hunters and gatherers to cultivators of the environment, technology provided twentieth-century workers with tools for conducting business, all of which made actual interpersonal contact less important.

Many of the investment firms that are around today have been around since the time of Baby Boomers and Gen Xers, making these two generations their target markets. So what did investment firms do? They did what any sensible marketer would do: They started pitching to and communicating with these generations in the manner to which they were most receptive. It worked, and that is the way they have been doing things ever since:

- Sending emails with PDF attachments

- Selling to analysts face-to-face

- Having little to no content to share (the best, however, utilized magazines, direct mail, PR, etc—all precursors to the modern-day Internet and content marketing)

- Answering questions as they come up

- Using technology minimally, if ever, and focusing on the path of least resistance

The problem now is that times have changed. We now live in an interconnected world where everyone has access to any information they need at any time because we live in a Content Economy. What is interesting to me is that, despite the reality of the Content Economy, many companies, and in particular, my world of investment firms, have not evolved their marketing approach to reflect how their current buyers buy (e.g., consuming high-quality content on your product).

Amazon, by the way, is the clear leader in this area providing high-quality, in-depth content on all of the products on their platform, including user reviews.

We have discussed the Content Economy superficially, but now that we have a good idea of the key players in the mix—this amalgamation of Baby Boomers, Gen Xers, and Millennials—it is time to take a more in-depth look at what the Content Economy is and what it signifies for our future. That is what we will do in the following chapter.

Key Takeaways

- ☑ Environmental factors influence key traits of each generation.

- ☑ Baby Boomers and Generation Xers used technology that is antiquated by today's standards.

- ☑ Both generations relied heavily on dialogue, whether in person or over the phone.

- ☑ Because many investment firms were born during the time of Baby Boomers and Generation Xers, their marketing practices still cater to these generations' preferences.

CHAPT

TER 3

WE LIVE IN
A CONTENT
ECONOMY

WELCOME TO THE CONTENT ECONOMY

Our economy and the purchasing decisions of every American is driven by the content they consume on a product, service, restaurant, hotel, car, etc. Rarely do people purchase anything without first checking it out online. We live in a Content Economy.

The Content Economy is an economy in which products are bought and sold using content with no interaction with a salesperson. As mentioned previously, Amazon is the clear leader in this area where all consumers can search and learn about products without having to talk to someone.

YouTube is the video content leader, but as of this writing (August 2018) what is emerging within YouTube is the massive growth of How-To videos. It is the fastest-growing segment of YouTube, growing eleven times in the past two years.[10]

We operate in an economy where authentic content, in the form of video, images, audio, reviews, likes, shares, posts, and in some cases text replaces much of the former face-to-face meetings and telephone conversations that took place during the course of economic history. Technology has enabled the rapid access to content of all kinds and has eliminated the need to speak with a salesperson. No one is calling Amazon to see if a book is in stock.

People search on Google and YouTube, read reviews on Yelp and Amazon, and listen to podcasts or read a blog, among many other things.

---

10   "Watch time of "does it work" videos grew by more than 11x in the past two years," Think with Google, https://www.thinkwithgoogle.com/data/does-it-work-youtube-search.

This content helps consumers connect with the manufacturers in a more meaningful way to help make a decision on whether or not to buy, what to buy, and then how to use it.

Whether this is a good or bad thing isn't relevant or a topic of this book. The point is, if you want to compete in this economy, you must be thinking about creating content or creating content on your product that allows buyers to connect with you on their own time. What I have seen from all my research for this book is that the people who are willing to share and open up their lives to their buyers are the ones who are literally skyrocketing their careers and businesses.

> WHAT I HAVE SEEN FROM ALL MY RESEARCH FOR THIS BOOK IS THAT THE PEOPLE WHO ARE WILLING TO SHARE AND OPEN UP THEIR LIVES TO THEIR BUYERS ARE THE ONES WHO ARE LITERALLY SKYROCKETING THEIR CAREERS AND BUSINESSES.

One person I follow extensively and who is the leading online marketing guru and sales funnel expert is Russell Brunson and his Click Funnel empire. He brings value to his followers and creates authentic content constantly and invites you into his life. He is really spectacular at it.

I'll say this repeatedly throughout this book: Boomers and Xers and anyone else who want to connect their firm and products with today's consumer must become a *content creator*.

Much of this content is available through technology, including social media, but I maintain that the Content Economy is not just about social media. It's about the consistent creation of content to allow consumers to connect with you on their own time.

We commissioned a study performed by Jason Dorsey and his team at the Center for Generational Kinetics. One of the key questions that they asked of 1,011 Millennials, is how important content was in terms of their opinion of a company. The response was scary: 57 percent said they don't trust companies if they cannot view content and **23 percent said they believe a company is hiding something if they cannot find any content on them.**[11]

Here's how the creation of content enables consumers in the Content Economy:

- It allows for self-education.

- It allows the seller to always put their best salesperson (their content) out front.

- It allows for sharing and liking.

- It allows for feedback, which leads to improvements

- It allows for the holy grail: data analytics (no content, or no analytics).

- It makes the buying process easier.

- It allows for greater transparency.

- It allows consumers to develop their relationship with you, in turn, breeding familiarity, trust, and connection.

---

11   See Appendix.

- Here's the equation for good content: content = user engagement = sharing = liking = data analytics = improvement.

Without content, you don't get any of the above benefits.

WINNING IN A NETWORK EFFECT ECONOMY

What's really important to realize is that the Content Economy isn't something that's about to happen or will happen in the distant future. It's already happened and continues to happen.

In fact, by changing your behavior—which is difficult—and taking action now, you're not beating the curve, you're catching up. The changes have already happened. Companies and businesses are either (a) already creating content; (b) just now experiencing the dawn of realization and making preparations to adapt; (c) sticking their head in the sand and don't understand what is happening today; or, (d) refusing to change because they are old and don't want to adapt.

You do not want to be in those last two categories, because this could be a matter of the longevity of your business. There's too much at stake.

Content is what's driving purchasing decisions. The companies that create the best content connect better with their customers and make the buying decision easier. They bring their products into their lives. Failing to address the creation of value-added content versus promotional content is what separates the good from the great or, even more dramatically, the ones who survive or dominate an industry.

MILLENNIALS ARE NOT ALIENS

As mentioned previously, we commissioned a study recently by the Center for Generational Kinetics (CGK) to reveal trends and to uncover the primary drivers behind Millennials' purchase decisions. To facilitate this study, CGK and Dakota Holdings designed a custom, twenty-seven-question survey. The survey was administered to 1,011 US respondents between the ages of twenty-two and forty and who had made an online purchase in the past three months preceding the onset of the survey.

The results of the study speak to the trends I discuss in this book. As you can see in the chart below, most Millennials prefer a mix of in-person and online purchasing. While some prefer to buy more items in-person, others are more likely to prefer an even split.

PREFERRED METHOD OF BUYING

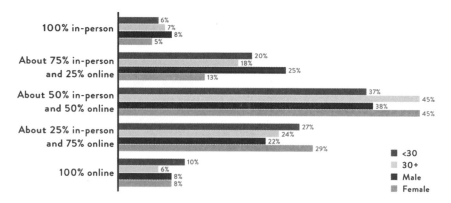

However, over two-thirds of Millennial shoppers would ideally like an important purchase experience to happen online. In fact, those aged below thirty and women are more likely to prefer a fully online purchase experience. The graph below shows the ideal purchase experience desired by this group.

IDEAL PURCHASE EXPERIENCE

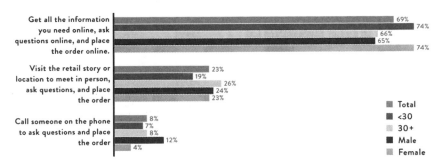

The study also showed that over the last year, almost two-thirds of Millennials have increased their number of online purchases. Millennials making between $75,000 and $99,000 a year have found themselves making more purchases online over the last year compared to those in any other income group. Another interesting finding is that over half of the Millennials have decided against a purchase that make them pick up the phone or meet in person. In fact, nearly half of the Millennial shoppers surveyed said they feel annoyed when a purchase requires a call or visit.

The study found that Millennials tend to feel frustrated if they can't access the information they need online in order to make a purchase. They may also feel that companies without an online presence are out of date or even suspicious. They may even lose trust in a company with limited online information.

One of the most striking results from the survey regarded the importance of online content in making decisions. Two-thirds of Millennials surveyed feel that online content is important or very important when making an important purchase. The study showed that companies with readily available online content are dramatically more likely to get Millennials' business.

IMPORTANCE OF ONLINE CONTENT WHEN MAKING AN IMPORTANT PURCHASE (BY TOTAL)

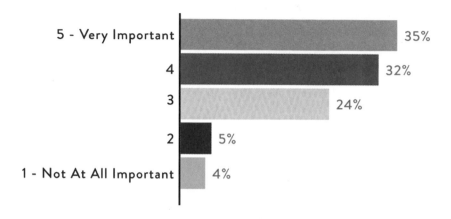

In conclusion, the study states: "Millennials have increasingly adapted to making online purchases and rely heavily on online content when researching about product information, purchases, and to inform buying decisions. They highly value authenticity, are trusting, and accord more value to user-generated content compared to any other type of content. As such, product manufacturers and dealers need to have an established online presence through which they can engage their target customers in order to tap into the Millennial customer pool."

A DAY IN THE LIFE OF A BUYER IN MY INDUSTRY

I am a sales and marketing professional in the investment management industry where I raise capital for a variety of different investment strategies.

A colleague recently told me that the investment industry, from a sales approach standpoint, is stuck in a World War I era, meaning very little has evolved for how we market our products (e.g. strategies). Currently, 100 percent of salespeople in the investment business communicate with their prospects and clients using email and PDF attachments, which, given the amount of emails prospects receive and how few emails ever get opened or read, it's amazing that they haven't thought of anything more innovative or new.

And we conducted an informal study and interviewed over two hundred institutional investors and simply asked how many emails they receive a day and if they read them. The answers were very similar. "We get so many on a daily basis we simply don't read or open them."

> **And we conducted an informal study and interviewed over two hundred institutional investors and simply asked how many emails they receive a day and if they read them. The answers were very similar. "We get so many on a daily basis we simply don't read or open them."**

So salespeople just inundate these buyers with emails and attachments and think that someone will react.

The following scenario could happen in any sales situation. I just wanted to use an example from my industry to show exactly how inefficient current and past processes really are.

Jennifer is a portfolio manager for a mid-size investment firm. She's meeting with Bob, a due diligence analyst who works for a bank that has a $12 billion wealth management unit where he reviews different investment ideas for their clients' portfolios. Jennifer's job is to introduce her firm and strategy and answer all the normal questions she, for the most part, knows that Bob will want to know.

Bob's job is to learn an in-depth amount about Jennifer's firm and strategy, analyze its risks, and compile information for a potential investment committee presentation where he will present the strategy. But first he has to like it enough to want to present it to the committee.

Jennifer leaves the meeting and does what every other portfolio manager and salesperson does: She sends Bob an email that goes something like this:

Bob, thanks so much for taking the time to meet with me. As a follow-up, I have attached three PDFs that will answer the questions that you had regarding our investment strategy. On the Strategy Overview PDF, the slides that answer your questions are on pages seventeen, twenty-four and thirty-one. I'm happy to set-up a follow-up call to discuss.
All the best,
Jennifer

This is the standard operating procedure for 100 percent of all people selling a product and following up after a call or a meeting, regardless of industry.

Salespeople fail to realize, especially in our industry, that the buyers receive hundreds of emails a day and they will admit to you, if you ask them, that they generally only read the most important emails and all the others go unread or get lost.

How many people actually open the PDF and turn to page thirty? Few, if any, according to over two hundred interviews we did with investment analysts.

What does this all mean? Buyers, regardless of industry, are inundated with emails and attachments. They are poor content managers, which is what we as salespeople turn them into because of how we approach them.

Amazon has done the reverse since they started the company. They amass a lot of high quality content on each one of the products on their platform, both firm related and user-generated, all in one place. So if I am to buy something on Amazon, I don't have to worry about where I put what emails, PDFs, videos, podcast, etc. They are all in one place all the time for me to go back to and review. The key is that you can literally put an unlimited amount of content in that "one place" far greater than any email could accommodate.

So, what potentially could Jennifer do to make it easier for Bob to learn about her product and review content on his own time? She could put all of her product content in one place, including all PDFs, video, audio, any quarterly updates, webinars, bios of team members, etc. Then Bob would know over time the one place he could go to get information on her strategy.

At our company, for investment firms, we have created that "one place" to post content, called the Stage Investor Network, where investment professionals can view at any time.

But for the most part, this practice is not de rigueur because there's a major flaw in the industry's content creation process.

For a small firm, thinly staffed with marketing professionals, the resources to create compelling content that answers the numerous key questions of due diligence analysts are simply not available.

To return to the case of Jennifer and Bob, the approach does not make sense. Bob has the capital to invest. He has the need and he has the authority, yet he is the one doing all the work on the strategy for which Jennifer is hoping to collect fees. Shouldn't the "seller" do more of the work for the buyer?

There are market forces changing the landscape as well. In our direct sales business, we regularly speak with due diligence analysts and, although I can't quantify the numbers, we know anecdotally that the number of due diligence analysts have been reduced and that there's consistent turnover.

This leads to restarting sales cycles, which means we're only adding to an already spiraling problem.

There's limited free due diligence level content on firms and investment strategies.

When content is available, it's in the form of a Request For Proposal (RFP) (which have compliance-heavy language and content that's not written as it's pitched), pitch decks (which need to be interpreted), and fact sheets (that provide the very basics).

To get due diligence level content, buyers generally have to pay high fees to access a database.

Even with access to a quantitative database, there's a lot of time that must be invested in researching and reviewing materials to create an investment summary for an investment committee to make an informed decision.

You might argue that Jennifer was thoughtful to offer a follow-up call and also to offer to meet in person so Bob would not be forced to do extra research or pay to access a database. But that does not solve

Bob's diligence issue, which a package of diligence written from Bob's point of view would help alleviate.

THE RISE OF THE MILLENNIAL BUYER

There's another market force that's at play in the prior scenario: A larger and larger percentage of all buyers in our economy are Millennials. As both Boomers and Millennials age, Millennials are replacing Boomers and are the defacto buyer. As of 2017—the most recent year for which data are available—56 million Millennials (those ages twenty-one to thirty-six in 2017) were working or looking for work. That was more than the 53 million Generation Xers, who accounted for a third of the labor force. And it was well ahead of the 41 million Baby Boomers, who represented a quarter of the total. Millennials surpassed Gen Xers in 2016.[12]

And Millennials, as we've established, have very different buying behaviors than Gen Xers and Baby Boomers.

According to a study, 73.7 percent of Millennials said they would rather text versus talk to someone.[13] They like to search, browse, text, and email. What they don't prefer is talking to people. In fact, in another study, 75 percent of Millennials said they'd choose a phone that could only text over a phone that only could call.[14] Just look

---

12 Richard Fry, "Millennials are the largest generation in the US labor force," Fact Tank, Pew Research Center, April 11, 2018, http://www.pewresearch.org/fact-tank/2018/04/11/millennials-largest-generation-us-labor-force.

13 Liveperson, "Gen Z and Millennials now more likely to communicate with each other digitally than in person," PR Newswire, October 17, 2017, https://www.prnewswire.com/news-releases/gen-z-and-millennials-now-more-likely-to-communicate-with-each-other-digitally-than-in-person-300537770.html.

14 "Why millennials still love text," Open Market, 2017, https://www.openmarket.com/resources/millennials-still-love-text.

around you at your Millennial friends, kids, or grandchildren. They communicate very differently from prior generations.

The in-person sales practices of the past are not part of a Millennial's daily life, meaning that the thought of getting on yet another call with Jennifer or trekking across town to meet her to discuss the same strategy is not how Bob prefers to work. Millennials like to educate themselves and do their own research—on their own time—as we learned in Chapter 1.

They prefer accessible content and rely heavily on this content to make purchasing decisions.

HOW INVESTMENT FIRMS AND ANY BUSINESS CAN MAKE IT THROUGH

If boutique investment firms wish to survive into the future, they have to stop, listen, and take corrective action. They have to get into the mindset of a Millennial buyer and sell to them in a way that they want to be sold to. I believe the stakes are very high if firms don't adapt.

Course correction starts from the client-facing mindset of an organization. As I have explained, this is a tiger-changing-its-stripes type of challenge. Why?

Because investment firms are run by Gen Xers and Baby Boomers who like to talk versus text, read versus watch, use a desktop versus using a smartphone, they are the exact opposite of the Millennial buyer.

However, that is not the issue. The issue is that the Gen Xers and Baby Boomers are not naturally inclined to create the content the buyers (the Millennials) want to consume. It's a manufacturing issue.

So what needs to happen?

Gen Xers and Baby Boomers have to begin to develop a mentality to create content to allow their prospects and clients to engage with them and get to know them: video, audio, and well-written narratives to better connect their firm, products, and story to the Millennial buyer.

These leaders have to begin to put these changes in place moving forward.

Connection is more and more coming from content consumption than it is from human interaction or face-to-face meetings. That is our new world. Anyone under thirty-five connects with everyone and everything through their smartphone through videos, images, and texting.

> **Connection is more and more coming from content consumption than it is from human interaction or face-to-face meetings.**

But that's easier said than done because: "Pick up the phone! It's not going to dial itself," or "go see them," are the common calls to actions with the old guard in the investment business. The idea of creating a video or producing an interview that encapsulates a firm's strategy, team, or unique proposition is a foreign concept. Most leaders in these firms have had success raising money and they instinctively return to what they know, best summarized by the Greek poet Archilochus and later co-opted by the US Navy SEALS:

"We don't rise to the level of our expectations, we fall to the level of our training."[15]

I believe the issue any small to midsize firm faces in making content creation a priority is that they have an investment excellence culture and believe if they deliver returns investors will find them. While that is unquestionably the right ethos for a firm to have, I believe you need a dual sales strategy, that is 1:1 and 1:10,000.

The problem is exacerbated by the fact that an active manager's biggest threat—passive investing—is simple to understand, is easy to explain, is easy to track, performs well, and is cheap. That's a pretty good competitor. Passive investing uses its "ease of use" as a critical selling point. Active strategies are harder to explain, harder yet to understand, and harder to report on.

So how do you adapt?

First, get the reality of where we are today. The Millennial population is only becoming a bigger and bigger part of our economy each day. The Internet is not going away. Smartphones are only getting more powerful and more useful. Millennial and Gen Z buyers are not going back to talking to people, reading, and using their desktops. Today, and every day forward, leaders of any organization are dealing with a completely different buying behavior than you've ever dealt with before.

Second, accept the fact that your buyers want to educate themselves on your product. They want access to in-depth, high-quality information.

---

15   Originally attributed to the Greek lyrical poet, Archilochus, 2016, https://www.goodreads. com/quotes/ 387614-we-don-t-rise-to-the-level-of-our-expectations-we.

Third, accept that the biggest pain point of your buyer is the exhaustive administrative work that they have to do to learn about you and then report on and track you.

Fourth, start using the technology that exists today to help you help your buyers do their job. Technology solutions that eliminate much of the administrative work for the due diligence analyst exist. Video is a prime example and one of the best ways to sell and deliver your message and content.

Fifth, get comfortable with the concept of video and do your first shoot: a thirty- to forty-minute interview for a portfolio manager as if he or she were in a due diligence meeting. Then cut it up into many two-minute clips: firm overview, investment philosophy, process, risk controls, portfolio construction, etc.

Make sure you're creating content that communicates the strategy and makes it easier to understand. If you're seeking to be competitive in a more disaggregated world with a buyer who has different buying habits, your investment strategy content needs to adapt. And by that, I mean you need compelling content that allows sophisticated investors to learn a lot about your strategy on their terms and on their time, without having to speak with you.

If you allow the buying process to remain the same, it can only limit the number of prospects you'll engage. Buyers will seek other firms who can perform and whom they can get to know. Do more of the work for the buyer if you want to engage more prospects and give yourself more opportunities to raise capital.

All the best salespeople, especially in a technical sale, are the ones who dig the deepest and provide the greatest level of insight for their clients, doing something the client doesn't have time to do or showing them something they couldn't otherwise see.

GETTING YOUR CONTENT RIGHT

By now you understand that we're living in a world of Millennial buyers who are drawn to digital content, but primarily video and audio content. The most effective content is video content that's more self-service and self-education driven.

Understand that we live in a Content Economy. Practices and tactics from previous generations are broken or don't exist anymore. The Content Economy has already created a new standard of how buyers use content to make purchasing decisions and connect with brands. It's inevitable that these new standards will become required throughout every industry.

Acceptance and change can be tough concepts to grasp for those of us who are of a certain age and have achieved success using the old model. We're used to doing things a certain way. That's why it can be tempting to continue using those same tactics and practices today.

As easy as it is to turn our backs on what we know, we can no longer afford to do so.

Key Takeaways

- ☑ We live in a Content Economy, meaning buyers' habits are influenced by readily available content that lets them avoid interacting with a person.

- ☑ To survive, every business must flex its content muscles by creating compelling content that is meaningful to the end user, mainly Millennials.

☑ Anyone who fails to generate the right content makes it difficult for buyers to buy, which means buyers are more likely to give up on you and turn to more consumer-friendly businesses that do offer great content.

☑ The business that makes it easiest to buy wins the largest market share. The rest merely survive or wither away.

CHAPT

TER 4

THE GREAT TECHNOLOGY DIVIDE

A professional due diligence analyst who works for a Chicago-based endowment was in the midst of diligencing an investment manager about their strategy.

In 2017, I was talking on the phone to an institutional investor who works for a Chicago-based endowment about the differences between Gen Xers and Millennials and she recounted a story that proved my statement. She said, "I love this investment manager, but I had three simple questions about their strategy, so I emailed him. Do you know what he did? He called me and I had to spend an hour on the phone with him. He could have just replied to my email!"

Yes, Millennials *do* prefer more efficient forms of communication (texting and email) versus talking.

And yes, the investment manager she was interviewing was a Baby Boomer.

Baby Boomers and Generation Xers prefer making phone calls over texting or emailing. Millennials don't.

This story portrays the great divide before us.

It describes, in a nutshell, how the generations are accustomed to communicating and it really only has to do with what they had as they were growing up. Baby Boomers had landline phones and relied on the US Postal Service. Gen Xers first had a landline phone, then the beginning of the mobile phone explosion, the US mail and then many grew up using email. Millennials grew up on texting, email, and smartphones—in addition to all the social media platforms and apps to stay in touch with their friends. The Gen Zs even more heavily weighted to social media to communicate with apps like Instagram, Snapchat, and Facebook.

The scenario above depicts the frustrations and tensions I witness routinely between these generations, how they diverge, and how their varying habits have delivered us at an impasse. And, as we've previously established, no generation is wrong. Each is just different.

No generation is wrong. Each is just different.

Each generation grew up in different landscapes and around different technologies that have influenced the way we interact with one another, with society, with technology, and even within the consumer market.

Baby Boomers and Gen Xers are just as comfortable, if not more, taking pen to paper than putting finger to iPad.

They are accustomed to strolling into brick and mortar establishments, browsing aisles and physically comparing products before making a purchase.

They are used to candidly lobbing questions at a salesperson before confidently stepping into the checkout line. And their habits have manifested themselves in ways that still affect business practices today.

But there is no pride in doing arithmetic by hand when a calculator or excel spreadsheet can do it quicker and more accurately for you. The same goes for product content. It is simply more efficient to produce quality content on products that allows users to deeply engage, especially when that content is exactly what consumers are thirsting for.

It is important to note that in my industry—the investment business—the human connection between the due diligence analyst (the buyer) and the investment firm (the seller) will always exist. The investors who hold the capital will always want to meet the wizard or the person making the investment decisions. It is part of compliance and doing their jobs. However, most of these newer buyers (Millennials) would prefer to be able to consume an in-depth level of content to learn about products *before* engaging with a salesperson.

Many businesses (including my own investment business), remains rooted in salesperson-centric model, with the expectations that you must talk to a salesperson to learn anything of value or depth about an investment product.

Think about that for a second. Can you imagine if you wanted to buy something in this day and age and the only way you could buy it would be to set-up a call or a face-to-face meeting to learn about the product? You'd laugh at them, but for the investment industry, it's par for the course.

The buying habits of these new investors are very different and are on the cusp of demanding that better content is available to them so they can do their own research on their own time. Investors don't have the time to meet with every salesperson in person. It's simply not feasible.

Take Amazon for example. This online retail giant has completely rewired decades' old shopping norms. With a few clicks on your PC, laptop, or smartphone, you can buy virtually anything and have it delivered to your doorstep the next day.

Checkout counters or salespeople are not needed.

Conversely, consider what happens when the sales of a Baby Boomer or Gen X-owned business starts slipping. Many business owners' or managers' response is to do what they have always done: advertise more, hire more salespeople, do more public relations. They default to what they have done in the past, but the numbers will show you that those mediums no longer deliver the results. To think that increasing the size of their salesforces is the attitude is just plain wrong, based upon the data.

The data will show that using content to educate your prospects on non-product-oriented information is the single way to establish you as the expert in your field. By creating online, digital content on your firm and products that allow potential buyers to connect with you, you increase engagement and conversion two to three times.

Deep and authentic online content allows you to do something that was not possible before: It allows you to put your best salesperson in front of your customers every single time. The best salespeople control the content.

And that *is* possible with content.

Creating compelling content is a lot like placing your best salesperson or the company's CEO right in front of every single client every single time. It can pitch your strategies, products, and services authentically. Another benefit about content is that you have the ability to test and retest engagement with your content to make it the most impactful it can possibly be as it continues to penetrate your targeted market.

Also consider this: Your best salespeople aren't able to reach your entire pipeline, as there is only so much time in the day. Content can always perform its very best but it needs to be created consistently and many pieces can last for years.

So not only is content creation a winner, but it also steals the show because it offers what regular sales tactics don't: feedback for improving your business model through the analysis of data. And you can collect this data through what's called user engagement.

UNDERSTANDING USER ENGAGEMENT

User engagement is exactly what it sounds like: how users engage with your content.

To make it more relevant to everyday life, think about what it's like when you visit your local hardware store. More than likely, you browse the aisles in search for something until, eventually, a salesperson asks whether there's anything he or she can do to help you. Deliberate for a moment on how you typically engage with that salesperson.

Say you are in the lightbulb aisle because you are on a mission to replace your home's lightbulbs with something that is both environmentally friendly but can also help save you dollars on your electric bill. You'll likely ask questions, probe about the benefits of one lightbulb over another, and ask for personal opinions or popular choices. The salesperson you're interacting with has a good idea about what you are looking for. He knows your preferences (energy savers), he knows what's important to you (economical consumption), and he knows what will turn you off (ridiculously high-cost bulbs), so he knows which product is best suited for your needs.

By engaging with him, you have provided a lot of useful insight that could help the company if they were to collect this feedback from all their customers and somehow compile and analyze it to modify their inventory based on consumers' needs.

But that feedback likely does not make it past the salesperson to directly benefit you or the vast majority of shoppers just like you in any way in the future.

However, what if it was possible to capture that feedback somewhere and use it to catapult improvements in your business? What if you could uncover precisely what your potential customers are looking for and work to deliver exactly that?

Online content allows you to do just that, using user engagement to test your customers' purchasing habits.

The fact is, everyone nowadays wants data analytics on users to diagnose how they are engaging with the proposed service or product. Data allows you to see correlations, to see where users are spending the most time, and to identify what they are not at all interested in.

For example, post content to your website and you become privy to all sorts of information—how many visitors are interacting and engaging with your content—whether they are sharing your links, commenting on your blog posts, and viewing your sales-driven landing pages. The dashboard of your website delivers numerous statistics and graphs so you can see the engagement of your content. Online tools allow you to analyze these engagements even deeper to see how long visitors watched your videos, how many pages of content they read in PDF viewer, how many seconds or minutes they spent listening to your podcasts, and how many—and what types of—questions they asked about your blog posts. And the neat thing is, each form of user engagement reveals something different about the success of your content. Let's take a look.

SHARES

Webpage widgets allow most blog posts and online articles to be shared throughout social media platforms like Facebook, Twitter, Instagram, and Pinterest. All it takes is a simple click of a button.

Generally, when your content is shared, it means that someone found it interesting enough to circulate it directly to their own social network, which says a lot. People only share the best, most valuable content, because even though it is your name on the article or content, it is their name behind the recommendation. Shares are great for businesses because they offer you free exposure. By viewing how many times your content was shared, you can learn a lot about your customers' most desired topics and notice trends in high or low performing articles to help you formulate or steer clear of similar content in the future.

LIKES

Many online articles allow you to show your appreciation for an article by clicking a thumbs up or "Like" button. When your audience takes that extra second to click that button on one of your articles, it means they connected with it positively on a personal level—whether they found it to be useful, entertaining, interesting, unique, or something else. Viewing how many likes an article has is a quick way to gauge what information or subjects people are most receptive to and can give you a good idea about what kind of content to devise going forward.

COMMENTS

Of all the engagement types out there, comments are perhaps some of the most valuable because they are feedback that is completely free of cost. By paying careful attention to how your audience is reacting through comments, you can learn a myriad of things. Sometimes people will pop in just to say that they liked your post, others may ask follow-up questions (which can cue you in about what other topics to cover in future posts), and still others may share their opinions. Receiving feedback like this is like engaging in a virtual conversation with someone who is willing and able to provide a tremendous amount of information that will help you determine hot-button issues, future topics, and even trivial things, like which writing tone your audience is most responsive to.

SUBSCRIBERS

The most coveted of all user engagement are email subscribers—content creators' best friends. When someone subscribes to your email list to receive regular communications and updates from you, that is the biggest testimonial to content success, because they're giving you access to one of their most prized and personal spaces of all—their inbox. Having email subscribers means having permission to be directly in people's inboxes anytime you want, which makes those people less likely to forget you and more likely to stay connected with your product or service.

Also, with your subscription audience, you have access to a whole new host of golden data such as tracking which subject lines have the best open rates, and how many of those opens result in click-through rates, or your subscribers heeding to your call to action (if you've included one in your email).

For those not familiar, a call to action (or CTA) is an action you want the subscriber to take as a result of their reading your message, whether it is to click on a link, download content, buy your latest product, or even simply reply to your email.

Shares, likes, comments, and subscribers are all user engagement types made possible through a combination of the Internet and the Content Economy.

However, it is important to remember that there are different levels of content. According to Adam Witty and Rusty Shelton in their book *Authority Marketing*, you have three types of content:[16]

1. Owned

2. Rented

3. Earned

If you have a sparse website that has nothing to download, no videos to learn something from, no podcasts, no images, no blog posts, etc., then you're stripping your engagement channels.

Without trackable digital content, your potential clients have nothing with which to engage. They have nothing to comment on, they have nothing to rate, and they have nothing to like or share from your site. This means you cannot get inside their minds to understand their thoughts. There is no way for you to determine what resonated with them, what they liked and what you should do more of, or what they did not like and you should eliminate or modify about your business or content.

USING BIG DATA TO MAKE BIGGER STRIDES

The benefit of technology and user engagement is that you can do more than just rely on shares and comments to draw conclusions about what is working and what is not. You can gather data from how users engage with your content or applications and use that data

---

16   Adam Witty and Rusty Shelton, *Authority Marketing: How to Leverage 7 Pillars of Thought Leadership to Make Competition Irrelevant,* (Charleston: ForbesBooks, 2018).

using artificial intelligence (AI) to make recommendations based upon where they are spending their time.

The most popular analytical tool is Google Analytics, which allows you to track in a variety of metrics how users are engaging with your content. With this information, you'll know where your users are spending their time so you can make adjustments on how to deliver your product or service in a better, more valuable way to your users.

For those of us still trying to get the hang of managing our own websites or even figuring out how to use YouTube, data gathering and analysis can sound intriguing and daunting. But in a month, a quarter, or a year from now, I am confident it is going to be as easy as using Microsoft Word. As I mentioned, analytical tools like Google Analytics, Buffer, and Cyfe are already making it simple for people to receive reams of analytics and research with minimal effort, and businesses are using this information every day to remain competitive. However, once your clients speak to you through user engagement and you have data, your job isn't over.

As Jeff Bezos aptly put it, "Amazon is a customer-centric company, but that does not mean all we do is listen to our customers and it ends there. Your customers are relying on you to innovate for them. So if you want to be a market-leading company, you have to take the onus and put your customer on your back and innovate for them in ways that they never considered to make their life more convenient or make their job easier to do."[17]

---

17   Edison Nation, "Talking Innovation and Entrepreneurship with Amazon Founder and CEO, Jeff Bezos," YouTube, April 15, 2011, 11:00, https://www.youtube.com/watch?v=_KEKkVrzeU8.

That is exactly what you will use data for—to innovate, to change—because that's what a client-centric company does. It creates. It leads.

They are depending on you to be the guiding light, the person in the miner's hat figuring out stuff for them to make their lives easier and more convenient.

That is where we are in the investment business. Our buyers don't necessarily know the exact solution that will make their jobs easier. They just know they have a problem. The macro problem is that because so little self-service content exists on investment products, their job is labor intensive filled with administrative work. Said another way: highly educated professionals are doing a ton of admin work which has led to burnout and high employee turnover.

Institutional investment analysts will not come out and tell us, without us asking: "Guys, it takes too much time to do all the work to learn about every strategy during a search, so with limited amount of time, I can only look at a limited amount of investment strategies."

However, if you ask them the direct question: "Would all of a manager's content all in one place with video, audio, narratives, webinars, and all presentations be helpful?" The feedback we received is a resounding, YES! They *want* content. They'd love to have that content to do research. They'd love to use that self service content to reduce the amount of time it takes them to learn an in-depth amount about an investment strategy.

The truth is, investment managers are in a symbiotic relationship with buyers. When your buyer succeeds, you succeed. Listen to them. Create valuable content. Point them to it. Use the data generated from user engagement—and then take it one step further by using it to create a place they don't even know exists but is exactly where they want to be.

> **When your buyer succeeds, you succeed.**

That place might be a murky, nebulous idea in your mind at the moment. You may not even be able to think of it off the top of your head, or you may be completely confused about what any of that even means, and that's okay. But start thinking in this line of thought because, as Bezos validates, this is the way exceptional leaders and innovators think.

Understand that it's important to create this content to generate user engagement to gather data to make improvements. You do not want to be left behind, which is what we'll get into next.

FALLING BEHIND

The headmistress for a private girls school asked me to come speak to her board and staff about the mindset of Millennials since most of the parents of the lower school students are Millennials. We were talking through the mindset of a Millennial and how to engage with them and I asked her about how they are using video (the preferred medium for Millennials). "We're thinking about doing some [video]," she said.

There are several problems with this scenario:

First, the evidence shows that the kids make the decisions to attend the school, not the parents. How do Gen Z kids engage? Video, video, video. To not have one video on the lower school section of your website is basically saying: "I do not want to allow you to connect with me."

I can only say with anecdotal evidence, but there seems to be a deeper divide between public and private school enrollment. One factor is clearly cost and the other factor could be due to the lack of online content to engage kids to convince them to get their parents to pay for it.

Without content, as the headmistress said to me, you have phantom visitors. These are visitors to the website who never hit a call to action button (or contact us). They browse the site, but the content is not engaging enough to take any action.

Second, this school's elementary school enrollment has been dwindling for some time now and they had no clue why. By waiting for the problem to become as critical as it had become, they had probably lost many of their customers to other schools who were already leveraging content to attract Millennials' kids.

Third, the decision makers and people in places of authority in this school were all in their fifties and sixties—Baby Boomers and Gen Xers who aren't used to thinking in terms of marketing using content—so they probably didn't even realize what a huge opportunity had escaped them.

Lastly, because they never put out any content, they failed to receive years and years of feedback that—had they captured it through user engagement and analytics—would have helped them continuously improve content to increase tours of the school (the highest correlation among all marketing efforts to enroll a new student).

Even private schools need to get deep into the content creation game.

You do not want to be the personal trainer who is out of shape. You do not want to be the website designer who has a crappy website. You represent your brand—so make sure you are doing it well, otherwise you cannot expect others to trust you with their needs.

If you have a desire to remain competitive, relevant, and client friendly, it's in your best interests to create content to connect with those customers, particularly Millennials. Creating this content is not a waste of time or superfluous. Creating this content is in your best interest. It's how your customers buy.

> **If you have a desire to remain competitive, relevant, and client friendly, it's in your best interests to create content to connect with those customers, particularly Millennials.**

But once you create that content and post it to your website or upload it on YouTube, remember that you've completed only one step in adapting to the Content Economy. That content then has to encourage your site visitors or content consumers to engage with you, which is step two. Once you bag user engagement, you're off to step three, which is analyzing data from that user engagement to figure out how to continue to grow and improve your business because that's what life and business is about: Change. Growth. Adaptation.

Those who fail to create content are failing to adapt to the Content Economy. And by doing that, they are all but saying that they have zero interest in growing or remaining relevant. Unfortunately, those are the very people who risk the most loss.

User engagement might sound complicated, especially if you've never heard of or tried to implement it before. But generating user engagement is not very difficult once you get going.

ACTION PLAN FOR CONTENT CREATION (TO DRIVE USER ENGAGEMENT)

Putting user engagement into practice with your business is actually quite simple. Like with most tasks that sound daunting or unachievable, the best way to approach it is by chunking the information into digestible bites.

This is how we did it. We either have 1) an investor who doesn't know us but wants to learn about us or we want them to learn about us; or 2) a client who wants to be updated.

The goal is to create easily accessible content on your firm and products.

There are four steps you have to take to create content for your investment firm and strategies:

First, you need a place to house the content. Obviously, I'd recommend our online platform, the Stage Investor Network, but you can upload to your website or to a data room.

Second, if you are using the Stage Investor Network, get your basis words and numbers inserted and uploaded.

Third, upload from your shared folder all existing and historic documents like facts sheets, newsletters, quarterly presentations, webinars, white papers, case studies, sample RFPs, and anything else you have created.

Fourth, take your time to start creating original content, including due diligence videos, audio interviews, and podcasts.

Start by putting everything you hope to accomplish down on paper in sequential order. For example, first on your list may be to create your own website. Number two might be crafting some alluring content that's sure to draw the attention of your target audience. If you're a business, your target audience will vary. If you're in the investment space, focus on creating content geared toward your buyer.

Continue listing out and prioritizing exactly what you want to accomplish and in what order, adding firm deadlines next to each task to hold yourself accountable and remain on a structured timetable to complete each objective.

Don't move on to the next step until you finish the one you're on and don't stop or give up.

BEFORE YOU PUT IT TO PRACTICE

So far, we've discussed some powerful concepts and insights into the changes we're seeing around us every day.

But before we jump into implementing any changes to adapt to the Content Economy, we'll need to lay a sturdy foundation, because no change is fully impactful without the correct mindset. So the very first step here before we begin to walk through the steps to show

how you can adapt to the Content Economy or take advantage of the benefits of data and user engagement, is to train your mind and mentally prepare it for what's to come. The Content Economy will require change, and you must be mentally and physically prepared for that change.

Think of the next chapter as the very first step in your journey. Of all the steps you're about to take, this is the most important, so give it your all.

Key Takeaways

- ☑ Adapting to the Content Economy means creating content and then using that content to generate user engagement.

- ☑ You can use the data generated through user engagement to identify patterns of your consumers, including which of your content they are most and least receptive to.

- ☑ Once you analyze your data, you should learn from it and use it to make improvements to your site to give clients more of what they want.

- ☑ Those who don't generate content and make use of technology like user engagement and its relevant data are at risk of falling behind the technology divide.

☑ No content equals no user engagement, which means no data, which means no improvements. If you don't improve, you'll end up falling behind.

CHAP

~ER 5

REWIRING YOUR MINDSET

In this chapter, we explore what one needs to do to begin to think about creating content for their business. It's hard to emphasize enough that this is a behavioral change and not a buy-in change, meaning the evidence supports the fact that content can significantly increase user engagement with your products. But actually creating the content, the video, audio, and blogs is no easy task.

Based upon the prior chapters and differences in how Millennials grew up, there are significant behavioral differences. I have a fourteen-year-old who talks into his phone all the time. It's not because he's on the phone with someone. He talks to text and issues commands by voice. I don't think I can even remember the last time I saw him using his keyboard.

I never quite understood why he did this until a recent conversation with my friend. I was out with my friend Ross, a Gen Xer, one day. He was fiddling with his phone when all of a sudden he looked up at me, flustered, and said, "You know, I just wish I had the Blackberry. It was so much easier to type with."

My mind instantly flashed to the image of my son talking into his phone. And a lightbulb went off. "Ross," I said. "Don't you think Apple is not so quietly telling us that we should be using voice commands and not our fingers with these phones? They're not exactly bending over backward to improve the typing experience. In fact, they're one neon sign short of screaming, 'How about just skip that step and use voice dictation instead.'"

Our society is evolving at a rapid rate and as one of our portfolio managers recently said in response to a question about the growth of the stock process of many growth companies like Amazon, Netflix, Google, Facebook, PayPal, etc: "We are not going to go back to writing checks."

We are not going to stop shopping at Amazon. We are not going to stop using our smartphones and we are not going to stop sequencing the human genome. All of us need to adapt with market, but change is risky. Perhaps the most difficult risk to manage is ego risk.

As with anything in life, it's all mindset.

We have seen anecdotally with the launch of our digital content platform that when we emphasize video too much with Baby Boomer clients it freezes them and truly freaks them out. We had one portfolio manager scream: "I will never do video!"

> VIEWERS RETAIN 95 PERCENT OF A MESSAGE WHEN THEY WATCH IT IN A VIDEO COMPARED TO 10 PERCENT WHEN READING IT IN TEXT.[18]

Change is the unknown and the unknown is intimidating. Every individual settles into a mindset or a way of doing things: a routine. As individuals collect into generations, there is at least some reversion to the mean across the population and certain behaviors become the norm. If you are a Baby Boomer, have you shot an iPhone video today?

Some generations are most comfortable using a landline phone, shopping in brick and mortar stores, or paying by check. For Gen Xers, homes without televisions were outside the norm. Millennials have made cord-cutters (i.e., those without a television and cable

---

18   Matt Young, "Looking at the Facts-Why Video Content Has the Highest Retention Rate," Pop Video, June 6, 2016, https://www.popvideo.com/blog/looking-at-the-facts-why-video-content-has-the-highest-retention-rate.

subscription) a substantial percentage of the television and cable target audience.[19]

If you've never used, nor are inclined to use, video to research or learn, you probably won't understand why anyone else would want to do those things either. Nor will you understand why it would be useful to create video yourself. Of course, limiting one's thinking to one's own view of the world ignores all of the other possibilities that are available. In a business that needs customers to survive, ignoring other points of view could be a dangerous posture.

Your view of the world or your belief in the way things have been done doesn't matter. Think about all the great business disasters like Blackberry not believing a touch screen was possible or the fact that Kodak had the digital camera technology in 1976 but never brought it out for fear of cannibalizing their own business, until of course the iPhone did it for them.

If you're stuck thinking how *you* have done things and what *you* prefer, then you are not thinking about how your *customer* wants things done or understanding the way they want to consume information on your products. You are being myopic instead of customer-focused.

George Welch, the hall-of-fame football coach at my alma mater, the University of Virginia, would famously tell his players a quote from entrepreneur Victor Kiam: "Even if you fall on your face, you're still moving forward."

So you are either getting better or you are getting worse.

Is there any better motivation to just start to try and create content that this new set of buyers want to consume?

---

19 "eMarketer Lowers US TV Ad Spend Estimate as Cord-Cutting Acceler-ates," eMarketer, September 13, 2017, https://www.emarketer.com/Article/eMarketer-Lowers-US-TV-Ad-Spend-Estimate-Cord-Cutting-Accelerates/1016463.

> **If you're stuck thinking how you have done things and what you prefer, then you are not thinking about how your customer wants things done or understanding the way they want to consume information on your products.**

In the United States, approximately one-fourth of the population are Millennials. It seems incredibly limiting to ignore 80 million people, but many businesses are failing to speak to them because the leadership of those businesses are stuck in the ways of the past.

In the investment business, we're particularly optimistic. Chief executive officers and chief information officers of boutique investment management firms who are from the Baby Boomer or Gen X era believe that if they just deliver performance, the world will find them and give them money. The focus is on the product and not on marketing.

Every single day, more Millennials are being placed in leadership roles at their firms and they will determine the success of businesses of every type. They will inevitably be the majority of primary decision-makers across the business landscape. It cannot be stated enough that this generation is going to determine the success of almost every business.

If you understand the significance of what's happening and are ready to take action, that's great. But before you understand or learn to sell to Millennials, you'll have to rewire your mindset. That's the very first step of the rest of your journey.

THE MOST IMPORTANT CHAPTER

At our company, Dakota Holdings, we have a philosophy called the Dakota Way or our "way" of doing things. As a Gen Xer myself, I have had to throw my hat over the proverbial verbal wall and start creating content.

We created a video studio to shoot video and record podcasts. However, doing it consistently is difficult, but we keep moving ahead.

We created a YouTube channel for Dakota Holdings. Who would've thought we would create a YouTube channel? Are you kidding me? Just a couple of months ago, this was a foreign concept.

We have created numerous ebooks and have launched a blog. Creating consistent content is no easy task. But we keep creating, not as fast or as proficiently as I'd like to us to, but we continue to do it.

Through these marketing strategies, we wanted to create the opportunity to allow you to take some action. I believe that this part is the hardest. Rewiring your brain to develop the habits of content creation is what this is all about.

Those willing to use that power, however, must take this most integral step in preparing for that something new by doing this: rewiring your mindset. This is certainly true of anything new in life, not just for embracing the Content Economy. So, be open to new ideas. The right mindset is like taking the governor off an engine. It allows you to race at whatever speed is required to win.

Changing the mindset is liberating because more opportunities are made possible. It is a portal and there must be recognition that there is no undoing it, no going back. Once the mindset change takes place and a commitment is made to travel in the direction of the Content Economy, new possibilities for business become possible. While discarding old habits or preferences can be difficult, I assure you it will be worth it and it will get easier as you keep going. Just don't stop.

I want to acknowledge this: Rewiring your mindset is not an easy task. It's a break from the known and the way things have been done. However, if you want to maximize your opportunities in a Millennial-led world, a change in routine, habit, and mindset is a must.

ADOPTING A MINDSET CHANGE

Preparing your mind is like ensuring that a home you're building is on level land and allows for a stable foundation. Just as one would not build a home without first excavating and leveling the land, one should never, ever, embark on building a mindset change without first excavating old, irrelevant ideologies and laying the proper groundwork for the new.

Everyone has either one or a combination of the two types of mindsets there are: a fixed mindset and a growth mindset.

The concept of a growth mindset is fairly well known. Professor and author Carol Dweck deftly explains the attributes of the growth mindset in her book *Mindset: The New Psychology of Success*. For those who have not read the book, I highly recommend it—it's an important companion to the points made in this book.

"Mindset change is not about picking up a few pointers here and there. It's about seeing things in a new way. When people change to a growth mindset, they change from a judge-and-be-judged framework to a learn-and-help-learn framework. Their commitment is to growth, and growth takes plenty of time, effort, and mutual support."[20]

GETTING STUCK IN A FIXED MINDSET

Let's say you have a friend who is pretty concerned about her son, Josh. "He's not doing too great in school," your friend confides in you. But my husband and I weren't the greatest students, either, so I guess I can't really expect much out of my son."

Your friend has a fixed mindset, meaning she views attributes, intelligence, and talent as fixed traits that are predetermined. People with a fixed mindset believe that everyone's talents and abilities are limited.

Common characteristics of people who have a fixed mindset include:[21]

- focusing on tracking successes and intelligence instead of discovering ways to develop that intelligence,

- being sensitive about being incorrect or making mistakes,

- seeking validation in everything they do,

- feeling self-doubt and eroded self-confidence in the face of failure,

- feeling anxious and disheartened by criticism,

- believing that talent, not effort, leads to successes, and

- believing that brains and talent are everything.

---

20   Carol S. Dweck, *Mindset: The New Psychology of Success,* (New York: Ballantine Books, 2012).

21   Reza Zolfagharifard, "Growth-Mindset Vs. Fixed-Mindset," Positive Psychology Program, February 8, 2015, https://positivepsychologyprogram.com/growth-vs-fixed-mindset.

People with a fixed mindset don't push themselves beyond their perceived potential to explore what could happen and what could be acquired. In short, these people tend to be stagnant in their ways and beliefs, and they don't strive for greater achievements.

Without the right mindset (one that is open to new possibilities), embedded and/or rigid beliefs can limit an individual, but if that individual is in a leadership position, their mindset can also limit their organization or even their family. Would you want your children to believe that their ability to achieve has been hard-coded and will never change?

A fixed mindset is an obstacle to goals. However, it is possible to adjust a fixed mindset to a growth mindset.

A fixed mindset is an obstacle to goals.

POSSIBILITIES WITH A GROWTH MINDSET

The counterpoint of a fixed mindset is a growth mindset. A growth mindset is a mindset that is open to the idea that skills and knowledge can be developed and honed. It allows individuals to learn skills and strategies to achieve the growth and progression that enables success. In other words, individuals with a growth mindset don't think intelligence is limited or preset. They believe anything is possible.

People with a growth mindset believe:

- abilities and smarts are achieved, not innate,

- any ability can be developed with persistence and hard work,

- brains and talent are part of success but not the ultimate determinant,

- good strategies and openness to criticism can improve and develop the individual and group,

- there is always an opportunity to improve,

- there is room to explore uncharted territory to expand abilities and knowledge, and

- failure or rejection is a temporary obstacle and a valuable learning experience.

A growth mindset is exactly the kind of mindset you want to have. It allows for growth and development, encourages the push required to meet goals, and instills confidence that obstacles can be overcome.

Most people probably fall somewhere between a fixed and a growth mindset. The key is to develop a stronger growth mindset. The more one practices, the easier it becomes to shed the fixed mindset and eliminate the noise and resistance that retards the progress toward goals.

In our example, a growth mindset will enable you to dampen the doubts about adapting to the Content Economy; that it is beyond current capabilities.

It is perfectly normal to have fears, apprehensions, or self-doubt. It's human. However, that fear cannot take over and prevent every attempt to achieve the results that matter. It's not okay when fear of change puts a business or livelihood at risk. A growth mindset will help eliminate that fear and self-doubt.

"Why waste time proving over and over how great you are, when you could be getting better? Why hide deficiencies

instead of overcoming them? Why look for friends or partners who will just shore up your self-esteem instead of ones who will also challenge you to grow? And why seek out the tried and true, instead of experiences that will stretch you? The passion for stretching yourself and sticking to it, even (or especially) when it's not going well, is the hallmark of the growth mindset. This is the mindset that allows people to thrive during some of the most challenging times in their lives."

Carol S. Dweck, Mindset: The New Psychology Of Success

As I mentioned, a shift in mindset offers benefits beyond just creating content. It offers the opportunity to have a more optimistic, opportunistic outlook on life. Knowing how important the right mindset is enables one to be more prepared and cognizant of possibilities before embarking on new challenges. It allows one to channel those thoughts in a more preparatory, positive direction to achieve the most from any effort.

For our purposes, a growth mindset propels one toward creating content to provide the opportunity to allow Millennials to better connect with your firm, products, and services.

Here are five mindset shifts I recommend to begin.

MINDSET SHIFT #1: SAY YOU *CAN*

I am not technologically savvy.
I do not know how to shoot video.
I do not know where to begin.
I am going to look silly on camera.

Some of these fears may sound familiar.

For every decision, the mind will trigger objections or fears. Am I paying too much? Do I really need this? The right mindset is the first step to fighting back. Defeat the fear by having an internal conversation about why a fear is only one possible outcome.

The mind is a self-fulfilling prophecy. If the focus goes toward what cannot be done, then that is exactly what will happen, nothing will get done. If the mind allows for new outcomes, those outcomes become possible.

For example, if a person is not tech-savvy and doesn't understand the first thing about coding, designing, or setting up a website, acknowledge that fact as a step to be addressed. Make an honest assessment and identify a solution. Find a resource that can overcome this obstacle.

If completing a task is being impeded, identify the bottleneck and take steps to remove the obstruction. This is particularly challenging for individuals in a leadership role, but humility is required. Delegate or hire the right resource to complete the task. Put people in roles that empower them to execute the plan.

> **If completing a task is being impeded, identify the bottleneck and take steps to remove the obstruction.**

Delegating is quite often the most viable solution for a lot of the hurdles an organization may face. In the case of reaching Millennials, there are probably Millennials already in your organization who can help with this task. While the organization is looking to leadership for direction, there's acknowledgement that the leadership won't be responsible for competing every task. Plenty of experts specialize in many of the things that require tackling, like developing a social media page for your business, promoting your website, crafting great content, and even creating a YouTube channel that draws viewers.

If money is a problem, devise a solution for that as well; set aside two hundred dollars every two weeks until you have enough available to hire someone to write blog posts. There's a solution for everything.

The job is to achieve the end objective: adapting to the Content Economy. It doesn't matter whether the efforts to get there are internal or external, made or bought, built by an individual or by an army. The end result is what matters, not the journey.

MINDSET SHIFT #2: TRY SOMETHING NEW

Old habits grow roots. If you want to push the possibilities for any enterprise, do something new, different, and impactful. For example, find one thing that can be improved, and brainstorm new or different or innovative ways of doing it.

Imagine a business that's accustomed to promoting itself through local value saver coupons and by distributing flyers at neighborhood stores. While effective at some level, those tactics are dated and are dependent on paper circulation (i.e., a cost driver). There's an opportunity here to research new ways to penetrate the target audience. A digital approach might be a cost-effective option that incrementally increases exposure. Groupon, AdWords, and Facebook are off-the-shelf options that might cover the existing base of customers *plus* expose the business to new clients who do not have interest in browsing through value saver coupons.

Sticking with the *same old* will deliver you the *same old*, and that cohort is getting smaller. New ideas and tactics offer the opportunity to bring new and often exciting results.

A word of caution here: Test before jumping in with both feet. For example, if passing out flyers—to use an old-world guerilla marketing tactic—has been working, it certainly isn't advisable to ditch that strategy and jump wholeheartedly into AdWords without validating the thesis. Instead, keep doing the flyers, but carve out some budget and time to explore the new idea. The focus should be on growth, not to demolish what has been created.

This idea behind this mindset shift is to introduce the idea of experimenting outside of the comfort zone and being open to new ways of doing things. Once the prospect of trying new things in small doses is comfortable, the bigger changes will not appear as intimidating as they once did.

MINDSET SHIFT #3: LOOK TO THE FUTURE AND PREPARE FOR IT

As I mentioned earlier, it's natural to become accustomed to routines without taking a step back to consider whether what's happening today is still relevant. Looking ahead forces one to think differently about each day, focusing more on how the present will impact the future.

Every day, the world changes a little. Many changes happen more gradually than suddenly, so it is important to always keep an eye to the future and be cognizant of the seemingly trivial tweaks and modifications taking place. Little changes add up to big ones, but it requires discipline to identify and examine the little things.

Analyze processes, benchmark against top performers, identify areas that can be improved, examine what can be done differently, and above all else, strive to understand what changes are already in motion that may have been overlooked. Get out of the day-to-day rut and build a culture that sees changes as they are happening or those that are just around the bend.

Know everything about everything that affects your business or industry. Network with leaders and colleagues in your space and attend industry-specific events. In the investment field specifically, think about the business as it relates to the most current generation of buyers, Millennials. Millennials are positioned to dominate the market for the next twenty years, but there will be a generation after Millennials and they'll have their own habits and norms.

Many people mistakenly believe that a seemingly insignificant change won't impact their business, or that they will somehow retire or escape before the change goes into full effect. That's a dangerous assumption. It's the root of the butterfly effect, which says the power to cause a hurricane in China can be attributed to a butterfly flapping its wings in New Mexico. The effect is not immediate, but the connection is real. If the butterfly had not flapped its wings at a specific place and time, the hurricane would not have happened. Small changes in conditions lead to drastic changes in the results.

While it's impossible to monitor every butterfly, it's not unreasonable to monitor the things that immediately impact your business. So make a plan. As Benjamin Franklin once said, "Failing to plan is planning to fail."

Kodak is an excellent example of how failure to monitor business conditions can have devastating consequences. The company invented digital photography and owned the technology for thirty years before any of its competitors.[22] Because the revenue and profits from print photography were so lucrative and because the company was so heavily invested into camera technology and manufacturing, it refused to promote or lead the transition to digital technology. Kodak was correct in that the margins for print were much higher (approximately 60 percent for print compared to 15 percent for digital), but they chose to focus on delivering quarterly instead of what was coming. Admittedly, the company believed the technology for digital was not practical or affordable for consumers, but there were plenty of examples in the consumer electronics sector (PCs, compact disc players, etc.) that indicated prices would fall and adoption would increase. By the time the world was ready for digital, Kodak started to adapt, but by then, it had missed its chance against its more eager competitors.

Although the company and its leadership saw what was coming, Kodak's short-sighted focus, coupled with its underestimation of the mass potential for digital photography, led to the company's demise. Decades of hard work, innovation, and the development of the Kodak brand were washed away. While Kodak certainly had a window to see into the future, the company failed to plan for it.

MIND SHIFT #4: THINK LIKE A CUSTOMER

Russell Brunsen, the founder and CEO of ClickFunnels, wisely said that you shouldn't price a product based on what you'd pay for it. Instead, you should price it based on what your customer would pay for it.[23]

---

22   "Kodak – A Case of Triumph & Failure," Manage Decisions, blogpost, October 26, 2010, http://www.managedecisions.com/blog/?p=444.

23   Russell Brunson, *DotCom Secrets: The Underground Playbook for Growing Your Company Online* (New York: Morgan James Publishing, 2015).

It's true that someone might be willing to spend a thousand dollars on something for which you wouldn't pay a hundred dollars. Individuals assign value based on their own criteria and everyone prioritizes value differently. The critical insight Brunsen observes is the need to evaluate everything from the consumer's view, not yours.

In order to put oneself in the customer's head, one has to know the customer, who they are, what they want, what they value, and what they don't.

All of us manage relationships all of the time, whether they're with siblings, parents, a spouse, partner, children, or coworkers. It's difficult enough guessing what people in your everyday life are thinking, but somehow, all of those relationships with their variations are managed.

In the same way, you have to understand the target prospect or consumer group when it comes time to develop content. You can't reach your audience if you don't know them. Everything from content delivery to tone depends on the target prospect or consumer group and what motivates them into participating and responding.

You may not make reading blog posts, listening to podcasts, or scrolling a Facebook page part of a routine exploration of a company, but Millennials do just that. It's what they do every day, so think like a customer and cater the messaging and the positioning of the business to the customer's needs. Break from the current mindset and reach out to the customer's way of doing things.

It's natural to wonder how to understand customers in the Content Economy. How is it possible to know what they want and how they want it delivered?

The answer, from the previous chapter, is user engagement. Through user engagement, it's possible to understand customers' needs and desires and to use that customer engagement and data to deliver to them exactly what they're looking for.

Technology and the Internet can be leveraged to learn more about certain customer segments and demographics which will aid in delivering meaningful content. Resources, all available on the web, exist to teach you about the customer base and how to best deliver value that matters to them.

MINDSET SHIFT #5: UNDERSTAND THAT THE CLOCK WILL NOT STOP

Of the five mindset shifts being proposed, the most difficult one to heed is that decisions are time-sensitive. The best of us hope for a few more minutes in a day or a few more hours in a week, but time has no pause button. Decisions have to be made and then executed. Time will not wait for a decision or a plan. The world will continue to progress with or without you.

The rise of the Content Economy is a testament to this fact. Millennials are already consuming content in a different way than any generation prior. This change has happened and there's no turning it back.

As you're embracing these mindset shifts, remember that retraining your mind requires practice, patience, and, above all else, ironclad commitment.

COMMITTING TO A FRESH PERSPECTIVE

We all make commitments in life—to our families, spouses, partners, children, and jobs or businesses. People commit to things that are important and meaningful to them. In the same way, you must make a commitment to changing your mindset, because delivering on that commitment will directly correlate to the health and success of your business.

When you're preparing a speech, it's not until that speech is practiced out loud that the words take shape and make sense. And then something magical happens. Those words become real, whether they're spoken in front of an audience of one or one million. If you're ready to commit to changing your mindset, say it aloud. Tell someone you trust that you're committed to a mindset shift. If you write it down somewhere (always a good idea), make sure to repeat it out loud on a regular basis so that it stays real.

WHAT IS AT STAKE

After reading this book and absorbing all the information, you'll have two choices: 1) to take the knowledge gained and do nothing with it, or 2) to embrace the change to benefit your business and your future.

If you choose the first option, you're taking a risk. Option one means not planning to change the way things are done. There's a lot at stake in failing to evolve a mindset. Consider where the world is today with Alexa, Siri, artificial intelligence, machine learning, and data analytics. Failing to change a mindset means failing to create content, failing to better connect with customers, and failing to generate and analyze data that leads to improvement. A mindset change is the first and most impactful domino that needs to fall before the rest follow. It is the pathway into the minds of Millennials.

Your lack of willingness to adapt to the Content Economy will only adversely affect you. Because others out there are ready to jump on the bandwagon—or already have—to deliver content in exactly the way Millennials desire. And many others will follow very soon.

Millennials are getting work done. They aren't tapping their fingers on their desks waiting for the world to catch up. That means others have adapted and are giving them what they want. Jump into their world and do the same before you become permanently irrelevant.

> **Millennials are getting work done. They aren't tapping their fingers on their desks waiting for the world to catch up.**

If fear or lack of ability is the obstacle, refer back to mindset shift number one: say you can. Countless numbers of people have adapted to this kind of change seamlessly, and they're reaping the benefits.

For now, remember that the mindset is the most critical component on which to focus.

Once the mind is prepared for the changes ahead, practicing a growth mindset should be routine, and embracing the five mindset shifts should be daily practice.

It will take practice and there will be stops and starts. There will be moments of hesitation, feelings of being lost, and self-doubt. Return to this chapter. Read it and apply it situationally.

I caution you not to move forward until all doubts, fears, apprehensions, and inhibitions have been set aside.

Once the mind is cleansed for a fixed mindset and in a sturdy place, the foundation can be poured. Remember a foundation sits best on excavated, level land, so prepare the mindset and adapt quickly and decisively. Those who do so are the greatest beneficiaries of the Content Economy.

Key Takeaways

- ☑ Before embracing change in any capacity, focus on having the right mindset.

- ☑ People with a growth mindset realize the greatest success because they believe talents and knowledge can be developed and are not fixed, predetermined abilities within humans.

- ☑ People with a fixed mindset tend to think abilities and successes are predetermined, which leads them to be less ambitious and more stagnant in their growth.

- ☑ To transform a mindset, focus on five key points:

    1. Say you can.
    2. Try something new.
    3. Do not lose sight of the future.
    4. Think like a customer.
    5. Understand that time will keep moving forward and the world will evolve with or without you.

CHAP

TER 6

GET STARTED

*"If you want to make an easy job seem mighty
hard, just keep putting off doing it."*

—Olin Miller

Think back to the first time you tried to jump into a cold lake. You were probably hesitant, wondering how you could get your legs to *just push off*, questioning whether swimming in such chilly water would even be enjoyable or bearable.

If you were unsure, you might have dipped one foot in and then the other before maybe jumping back out. If you were bold, you would have dove in cannonball style, taking your punishment all at once. In fact, most people will advise you to do just that.

This is the best analogy to describe how you should approach the next step of putting a plan into action: Just jump right in and get started. In fact, getting started is the single most important action you can take once you've prepped your mind.

Nike has built a juggernaut behind the slogan "Just do it." Interestingly, it was inspired by a convict's final words to a firing squad who were tasked with his execution.[24] When asked if he had any final words, Gary Gilmore said, "Let's do it." Nike was smart enough not to tie the brand to a serial killer and the modified phrase became a platform of inspiration for pushing their customers to pursue their dreams.

In order to progress, achieve goals, or accomplish anything, one has to take action. Getting started is an integral part of success, but the importance of action is often overlooked.

---

24   Marcus Fairs, "Nike's 'Just do it' slogan is based on a murderer's last words, says
      Dan Wieden," dezeen, March 14, 2015, https://www.dezeen.com/2015/03/14/
      nike-just-do-it-slogan-last-words-murderer-gary-gilmore-dan-wieden-kennedy.

We can assume that since you're reading this chapter, taking action should not be an issue. By now, you've tackled the prep work in Chapter 5, which is the most difficult step. The five mindset shifts are understood, practiced, embraced, and personalized, a commitment has been made to keeping an open mind, and a growth mindset has replaced a fixed mindset. With that, it's time for the next step—a step so integral that there's an entire chapter dedicated to it.

Many plan, prepare, and feel ready, but often that's as far as they get. Then comes paralysis by analysis. Procrastinating and failing to follow through on something is actually not unnatural or uncommon human behavior. In fact, it's common enough that it's been studied and coined the akrasia effect.[25]

The story goes that after much delay in penning *Hunchback*, Hugo was given a short leash by his publisher, who demanded a draft of the book in just six months. Hugo, who was easily distracted and prone to putting off writing due to his social engagements, is said to have locked away all his clothes except for a lone shawl in an attempt to avoid the temptation to leave his home. From there, he devoted his time to hammering out his draft and completed *The Hunchback of Notre Dame* two weeks before deadline.

Why do humans have this shared tendency to put off important tasks? There's a simple explanation.

The explanation theorizes that we delay completing tasks because of "time inconsistency," meaning that because the task we face usually benefits us at a later date, we don't see the urgency or importance to give it precedence over more immediate needs.[26]

25   Michael Pakaluk, *Aristotle's Nicomachean Ethics: An Introduction* (Cambridge: Cambridge University Press, 2005).

26   Jory Mackay, "The Important Habit of Just Sharing," Lifehacker, April 14, 2016, https://lifehacker.com/the-important-habit-of-just-starting-1771016698.

It would not be unusual to finish reading a chapter in this book and feel a genuine motivation to get started and begin implementing changes. However, it would also not be unusual to begin procrastinating when it's actually time to execute changes. Because there's no immediate reward for taking action now, it becomes tempting to push off the task.

Recognize that visceral instinct and avoid the trap of procrastination. Think of getting started as you would think of taking a trip in a car. The gas tank is full, the destination is loaded into the GPS, but until the car is en route, the planning and preparation is preamble. To reach a destination, someone has to turn the key and step on the gas. It's no different in business (or life). The mind's ignition must be revved and action must be taken.

Akrasia is real, and it can retard and delay you from taking action. However, there's a counter to akrasia, called enkrateia (from Greek), which means "being in command."

Practicing enkrateia and overcoming akrasia is easy once you know how. Here are some tips to getting started.

MAKE A COMMITMENT

Resistance to starting is grounded in the fact that some tasks, even after you start them, don't offer instant gratification. It could be days, months, or years before you actually see the fruits of your labor.

But there are also other contributing factors that could be hindering you: fear, apprehension, and confronting failure are just a few of them. If apprehension or uncertainty remain an obstacle, revisit the previous chapter and focus on preparing your mind to eliminate or at least set aside the obstacles that are stopping you from taking action.

Then commit to getting started. For instance, Hugo locked his clothes away so he wouldn't be tempted to leave home. That was his way of committing. This seemingly simple act forced him to start and, ultimately, complete his book.

For example, if your goal is to lose weight, you might commit by tossing all the junk food from your pantry. If your goal is to adapt to the Content Economy, you might commit by reducing the amount invested each month in the local value shopper or eliminating your worst-performing salespeople.

Actions are commitment "triggers" that help eliminate negative behaviors and prompt progressive actions. The cumulative effect is progress toward the end goal. As a junk food junkie, lack of access to bad eating choices will force more good food choices.

As a business owner, culling the salesforce will require subsequent action to make up for the lost salespeople, ideally in ways better aligned with the Content Economy. Creating an enhanced online presence might be a logical first step. Demonstrating commitment—especially when you're making a difficult or painful decision—supports a change in direction that will harness you to achieving a goal.

SHOW UP

Woody Allen famously observed that "Showing up is eighty percent of life."[27] It's the doing that makes the result possible.

Many of the goals you set will require repeated action. They can't be achieved in just one sitting. So make taking action a part of your

---

27   Susan Braudy, "He's Woody Allen's 1-1-Silent Partner," The New York Times, archive, August 21, 1997, https://www.nytimes.com/1977/08/21/archives/hes-woody-allens-notsosilent-partner.html.

daily routine. Getting started every day reduces akrasia, friction, and resistance to the act of starting. When performed routinely, getting started will become a habit and enkrateia will lubricate any doubts that persist.

> **Make taking action a part of your daily routine.**

REMOVE DISTRACTIONS

There's an irony to the distractions we face today: it's more than likely that the distractions of the Content Economy are the very deterrents blocking you from taking the actions needed to embrace that same Content Economy.

Showing up to the work is undermined by phones, social media accounts, blog post notifications, and news alerts. Be sure the environment for work time promotes productivity and limits distractions. Turn off the smartphone (better yet, put it away) when setting out to do something that requires full focus and attention, such as creating a website or writing content. Declutter a work area in the same way you've been advised to declutter your mind.

Bear in mind that the point here is not to finish the task, but simply to get started. Be encouraged with the small steps. As Confucius said, "The man who moves a mountain begins by carrying away small stones."

FORGET ABOUT PERFECTION

"A primary reason people don't do new things is because they want to do them perfectly—first time. It's completely irrational, impractical, not workable—and yet, it's how most people run their lives."

—Peter McWilliams[28]

It is tempting to strive for perfection. We're bombarded, from a young age, with stimuli stressing perfection. There's pressure to be perfect. Everyone on Facebook and Instagram seems to be living a perfect life. But as counterintuitive as it may sound, forget about perfection.

It is okay if an attempt at creating written content or video is a failure. It is okay if the first (or fourth) try at creating a robust AdWords campaign is a failure. The primary objective at the outset is to get started. Once action is built into a daily routine, there will still be plenty of time to learn, to sharpen, and to perfect. Perfection is not a reasonable standard to establish for early steps. Moreover, a standard of perfection is likely to result in two potentially crippling outcomes: 1) failure to see what *did* work as no attempt is likely to be an abject failure and there will be parts of any action that are worth building upon; 2) any level of failure will lead to discouragement and a temptation to give up. In the Content Economy, giving up isn't an option.

Focus on satisfaction with the process means: learning how to write content, learning the elements of a great video, discovering how AdWords works. Absorbing and observing the process is an accomplishment in and of itself. Focus on the small victories and under-

---

28 Richie Billing, "Procrastination: Dueling With the Devil," The Writing Cooperative, April 28, https://writingcooperative.com/procrastination-duelling-with-the-devil-de45a2775d2d.

stand that there's time to make improvements. The important thing is to take action and make getting started a habit and an integral part of your routine.

EXERCISE

Due to the fact that getting started is critical to reaching any goal, I've created a simple self-reflection exercise designed to provide you insight on your personal approach. Based on your responses, you may realize patterns of resistance and notice common obstacles that have historically prevented you from achieving your goals. To make the most of this exercise, be sure to focus on providing the most accurate, specific, and candid response to each question.

1. List the last three goals you set for yourself. Next to each goal, list obstacles that prevented you from getting started on attainment of those goals.

_____

_____

_____

_____

2. Did you overcome the obstacles? If so, how?

_____

_____

_____

_____

3. List the goal(s) you are hoping to work toward and potential obstacles that could prevent you from getting started this time.

_____

_____

_____

_____

4. How do you plan on overcoming those obstacles and managing resistance to starting?

_____

_____

_____

_____

NEXT STEPS

Hopefully by now you're starting to see the first glimpses of an action plan taking shape in your mind and feeling a sense of excitement about getting started.

In the next chapter, we'll talk about the single most effective way to dominate the Content Economy: by using video.

Key Takeaways

☑ Once the right mindset is in place, the most important thing you can do is get started.

☑ Procrastinating is a natural human tendency.

☑ People procrastinate because it's common to prioritize tasks that offer instant gratification over those that offer delayed or future benefits.

☑ Although getting started can be difficult, once they do, many people find that doing the task is less painful than procrastinating.

☑ A commitment to getting started is the first step to defeating procrastination. Committing means showing up, eliminating distractions, and accepting that outcomes may be less than perfect.

CHAP

ER 7

THE UNDENIABLE POWER OF VIDEO

I decided to make a separate chapter on video after doing our initial research. I was so blown away by the numbers and the magnitude of video I figured it made the most sense to completely expose the video statistics and story to my audience, so they can learn quickly what a powerful business, sales, marketing, and brand building video has become.

If the word "video" means television or a VHS tape to you, you've probably never posted a "story" of your meal on Instagram or uploaded something on YouTube. And if you aren't posting or sharing or uploading, you're most likely a Baby Boomer or Generation Xer.

You're not alone in your lack of experience with video. Asking people of a certain generation to voluntarily go on camera is less preferable to singing the Star-Spangled Banner in a swimsuit on national television. Conversely, Millennials devour video and have made it a part of their daily lives.

However anxiety-inducing it may be, getting on video and getting video out is an essential marketing strategy. The fact is, pretty much everyone under forty looks to YouTube to learn about anything they want.

THE RELATIONSHIP BETWEEN VIDEO AND SALES

As video is an extremely quick, easy, and passive way to consume information, Millennials rely on it as a starting point to develop an understanding about a product, service, or brand. Video has become such a powerful element of the buyer's journey toward making a purchase that it's considered the single-most powerful tool for marketing to Millennials.

Consider these statistics:

→ 95 percent of people have watched an explainer video to learn more about a product or service.

→ 81 percent of people have been convinced to buy a product or service by watching a brand's video.

→ 97 percent of marketers say video has helped increase user understanding of their product or service.

→ 76 percent of marketers claim that video has helped them increase sales.[29]

THE STATS ARE OVERWHELMING.

If you're still debating about whether to add video to your marketing strategy, consider this: Wyzowl says that **79 percent of consumers prefer watching video** to reading about a product.[30]

A NOT-SO-NOVEL CONCEPT

A quick history of recorded communication: Cavemen could not keep track of the count from the hunt by simply grunting and mimicking, so they took to cave painting. The caveman's epiglottis evolved and connected with the pharynx and larynx and the spoken

---

29   "Video Marketing Statistics 2018," Wyzowl, 2018, https://www.wyzowl.com/video-marketing-statistics-2018.

30   Sharon Hurley Hall, "Video Marketing Statistics: What You Must Know (2018)," OptinMonster, September 4, 2018, https://optinmonster.com/video-marketing-statistics-what-you-must-know.

word was born along with storytelling. This was only the beginning of evolution. Eventually there were books, then wired communications, then wireless communications, then radio and, finally, television. Man essentially did a round trip from sitting in the cave staring at drawings on the wall to taming the earth, discovering new lands, building societies, and advancing science—all for the luxury of sitting in a living room staring at the television against the wall.

Here's where that's brought us to today: the average person spends around ten hours and thirty-nine minutes per day watching media, of which television takes the lead.[31]

Television and video, in all of their forms, are uniquely pervasive. The technology has ventured beyond the confines of living rooms and bedrooms to the convenience of smartphone screens, tablets, and PCs. One fundamental difference, of course, is the opportunity to be the star of the screen. Millennials relish the opportunity to be seen in every way possible.

MILLENNIALS LOVE VIDEO . . .

It's worth exploring what it is about video that has Millennials fully converted and committed. Of course there's the obvious: it's passive, it offers creative expression, it's an easily consumable form of storytelling, and it requires minimal effort. On another level, though, video also allows Millennials to multitask.

The minimal requirement for complete focus is particularly appealing to Millennials. Other things can go on while video is

---

31   Jason Lynch, "US Adults Consume an Entire Hour More of Media Per Day Than They Did Just Last Year," Adweek, June 27, 2016, https://www.adweek.com/tv-video/us-adults-consume-entire-hour-more-media-day-they-did-just-last-year-172218.

playing or streaming. The same cannot be said of blogs or most other content-based materials.

→ 60 percent of Millennials prefer to watch a company video than reading a company newsletter.

→ 80 percent of Millennials use video to help them decide which products to purchase.

→ 85 percent of Millennials find product demos useful.

→ 76 percent of Millennials follow brands or companies on YouTube.[32]

Video is, hands down, the best way to connect with Millennials. Blogs and podcasts are great too, but are fighting for second place. Fifty-nine percent of senior executives agree that if both text and video are available on the same topic on the same page, they prefer to watch video.[33]

According to Arnold Street, Millennials are most responsive to visual stimuli.[34] Blogs and other digital-based materials may be packed with unique information and presented with exceptional quality, but it's video that gathers the traffic and views.

Consider this statistic I mentioned earlier: Videos are projected to claim more than 80 percent of all Internet traffic by 2019. Eighty percent is an unimaginably large share of the largest information

---

32   Nicole Dieker, "Infographic: Why Millennials Love Video Marketing and You Should Too," The Content Strategist, Contently, November 4, 2015, https://contently.com/2015/11/04/infographic-why-millennials-love-video-marketing.

33   Irfan Ahmad, "25+ Stats That Prove 2017 Is The Year Of Video Marketing – infographic," Digital Information World, December 13, 2016, https://www.digitalinformationworld.com/2016/12/infographic-video-marketing-statistics-2017.html.

34   "It's All About The Visuals: How to Target Millennials With Content," Arnold Street, June 1, 2016, http://arnoldstreet.com/visuals-target-millennials-content.

resource in the world and that's a 2019 estimate. Imagine what that traffic could look like over the following five or ten years. It's true that different media have come and gone (radio, newspapers, magazines), but video in all of its forms has been the primary killer of them. So it's safe to expect that it'll live on.

The best part is, the popularity of video is not confined to just Millennials.

. . . MARKETERS ALSO LOVE VIDEO

Marketers adore video just as much, if not more, than Millennials. When compared to other marketing strategies, video is extremely affordable to produce. Because it can be easily accessed, it's also an effective and powerful tool for marketing on a large scale. Plus, studies prove that viewers retain much more information from a video than from text, which makes it a better medium through which to showcase a product or service.

➔ 76 percent of businesses say that video marketing helped them improve site traffic.[35]

➔ 80 percent claim that video has increased the amount of time visitors spend on their site.[36]

➔ 76 percent of marketers believed that it's helped them increase their sales.[37]

---

35   "Video Marketing Statistics 2017 Survey: The State of Video Marketing," Wyzowl, 2017, https://www.wyzowl.com/video-marketing-statistics-2017.

36   Larry Smith, "60 Video Marketing Stats You Need to Know in 2018," Linkedin, April 11, 2018, https://www.linkedin.com/pulse/60-video-marketing-stats-you-need-know-2018-larry-smith.

37   Ibid.

Like blogs and podcasts, video can be easily shared with the click of a button, enabling the content to penetrate across networks of colleagues, friends, family, or even acquaintances. This drives efficiency in spending and delivers television-quality content without paying television advertising rates.

However, keep in mind that Millennials don't respond to just any kind of video content. Video must be relevant, qualitative, and provide valuable information. Putting thought into video content to make it stand out is crucial. Have a plan for look, feel, design, and tone.

WHERE VIDEO IS STEALING SCREEN

Gone are the days when video content was synonymous with only YouTube. Following YouTube's success are many others, meaning you can now find clips and films of commercials, tutorials, DIYs, and more, almost anywhere on the web, including on most social media sites.

YOUTUBE

Founded in 2005, YouTube was created by a trio of former PayPal employees as a dating site, allowing people to post videos introducing themselves to prospective dates. Like so many Internet-based ecosystems, the site morphed into something else and was eventually opened up to all types of video content.

Now the largest video site in the world, YouTube has more than a billion users and that's equal to almost one third of the total number of Internet users in the world. According to eMarketer, it's still the most popular place to share video, with Facebook following closely behind.[38]

From DIY videos to reviews to news, YouTubers use video to cover every conceivable topic. The site makes it easy to share videos with friends, leave comments, and even follow or subscribe to favorite channels and YouTube personalities. A handful of users have even launched themselves to stardom, kick-starting careers like those of Justin Bieber and Michelle Phan.

For marketers, on the other hand, YouTube is a still-emerging goldmine of opportunity. An article by Brandwatch lists statistics showing how YouTube is reaching the population:

➔ In an average month, 80 percent of eighteen- to forty-nine-year-olds watch YouTube.

➔ In 2015, eighteen- to forty-nine-year-olds spent 4 percent less time watching TV, while time on YouTube went up 74 percent.

➔ On mobile alone, YouTube reaches more eighteen- to forty-nine-year-olds than any broadcast or cable television network.

➔ YouTube can be viewed in a total of seventy-six different languages (covering 95 percent of the

---

38   Anmar Frangoul, "With over 1 billion users, here's how YouTube is keeping pace with change," CNBC, March 14, 2018, https://www.cnbc.com/2018/03/14/with-over-1-billion-users-heres-how-youtube-is-keeping-pace-with-change.html; Rahul Chadha, "Marketers Think YouTube, Facebook, Are Most Effective Video Ad Platforms (Surprise!)," eMarketer, January 29, 2018, https://www.emarketer.com/content/marketers-think-youtube-facebook-the-most-effective-video-ad-platforms-surprise.

Internet population).[39]

With advertisements prefacing nearly all of its videos, YouTube provides a unique chance for companies and brands to steal a bit of screen space on users' channels to promote a product or gain exposure and awareness for brands. Its effectiveness, particularly with Millennials, is why many advertisers are opting to pour money into this type of vehicle over more traditional advertising methods—Millennials do prefer YouTube two to one over traditional television.[40]

Millennials are not the only generation to enjoy the site. People between the ages of thirty-five and fifty-five are the fastest-growing YouTube demographic, meaning the popularity of video is fast spreading.[41]

FACEBOOK

Recognizing the power of video and not conceding the space to YouTube, Facebook launched its first video capabilities in 2007. Today, it ranks with YouTube, claiming more than eight billion average views a day.

---

39   Kit Smith, "39 Fascinating and Incredible YouTube Statistics," Brandwatch, April 12, 2018, https://www.brandwatch.com/blog/39-youtube-stats.

40   Salman Aslam, "YouTube by the Numbers: Stats, Demographics & Fun Facts," Omnicore, February 5, 2018, https://www.omnicoreagency.com/youtube-statistics.

41   "The Lastest YouTube Stats on Audience Demographics: Who's Tuning In," Think with Google, https://www.thinkwithgoogle.com/data-collections/youtube-viewer-behavior-online-video-audience.

After the success of video on its platform, Facebook has continued to expand its video endeavors with products like Facebook Watch. This video-on-demand service allows users to discover new shows based on what friends and others in their networks are watching. In essence, it seeks to offer the best of all worlds, a combination of YouTube, Twitter, and traditional television. Facebook has also launched Facebook Live, a live-streaming feature for users, similar to Periscope. Forbes says Facebook Live "has the potential to change the way marketers and consumers approach the platform—not to mention influencing most of the platform's contemporaries."[43]

LINKEDIN

Although LinkedIn is not considered to be a video giant like Facebook or YouTube, it's still a highly effective space for video content. At its core, LinkedIn is a refined social media site for professionals to connect and network with one another. When it started, LinkedIn allowed users to post and read content, but like many of its fellow social media platforms, it too has adopted video capabilities. Today,

---

42 Alfred Lua, "50 Video Marketing Stats to Help You Create a Winning Social Media Strategy in 2017 ," February 16, 2017, https://blog.bufferapp.com/social-media-video-marketing-statistics.

43 Jayson DeMers, "Facebook Live: Everything You Need To Know," *Forbes*, April 26, 2016, https://www.forbes.com/sites/jaysondemers/2016/04/26/facebook-live-everything-you-need-to-know/#3a12f25a55f2.

you can't scroll through a LinkedIn feed without encountering a video clip. Users take advantage of this tool to create quick intro videos for the benefit of headhunters and recruiters, promote products, boost brand awareness, or spread messages. Both professionals and marketers find the video tool to be an effective marketing strategy.

> ## 38 PERCENT OF MARKETERS HAVE PUBLISHED VIDEO CONTENT ON LINKEDIN OUT OF WHICH 75 PERCENT FOUND IT TO BE EFFECTIVE.[44]

Because LinkedIn is considered a social media site for professionals, the concepts of simple language, easy-to-understand content, and brevity apply. Lengthy blocks of text are a turn off, making video ideal for conveying technical or content-heavy information, think company reports, performance summaries, and the like.

TWITTER

A quick way to share brief thoughts with a network of followers, Twitter is known for its short, impactful, limited-character messages. Like other social media sites, it now offers video tools to let users "tweet" and share events in real time, create awareness about a subject, educate people, or promote a product or service. Similar to its text content, video clips are also restricted in length, not to exceed 140 seconds. Data indicates that Twitter video content is much

---

44   "How Brands Can Make the Most of LinkedIn Video in 2018," Wyzowl, 2018,
     https://www.wyzowl.com how-brands-can-make-the-most-of-linkedin-video-
     in-2018.

more impactful, boasting many benefits for marketers like two and a half more times more replies and two and eight-tenths times more retweets.[45] In addition, 82 percent of users are known to watch video content shared on Twitter, creating a promising way for marketers to increase their outreach on this platform.[46]

Like Facebook, Twitter has kept a keen watch on video to see where it can create enhancements for users. Most recently, an article in *Bloomberg* claimed that Twitter was in the midst of creating a new Snapchat-like technology to make it easier for users to use video on its app, which will likely pave way for marketers to benefit as well.[47]

INSTAGRAM

Instagram is more than just a visual storyboard that allows users to share life experiences through photographs with those in their network. Its video feature allows you to upload videos to a storyline, enabling businesses to make audiences aware of limited-time offers, attach a story to a brand, do a quick product demo, add a human touch to a company story, or even create a quick commercial.

---

45 Dominique Jackson, "A Comprehensive Guide to Mastering Twitter video," sproutsocial, January 28, 2016, https://sproutsocial.com/insights/twitter-video.

46 Mary Lister, "37 Staggering Video Marketing Statistics for 2018," WordStream, July 25, 2018, https://www.wordstream.com/blog/ws/2017/03/08/video-marketing-statistics.

47 Selina Wang, "Twitter Is Working on a Snapchat-Style Video Sharing Tool," Bloomberg, January 25, 2018, https://www.bloomberg.com/news/articles/2018-01-25/twitter-is-said-to-work-on-snapchat-style-tool-for-video-sharing.

> ## 25 PERCENT OF INSTAGRAM ADS ARE SINGLE VIDEOS.[48]

Adding a creative caption to your video along with relevant hashtags will place the video in a searchable category and allow it to surface as a result during relevant searches.

VIDEOS, MOBILE PHONES, AND MILLENNIALS

The age of video is obviously established. In addition to Millennials, there's another dominant force pushing video to the forefront: smartphones. According to Nielsen, over 85 percent of Millennials own smartphones, and if they're going to watch a video it's almost always going to be on a smartphone. According to YouTube, mobile video consumption is growing by 100 percent every year.[49]

> ## MILLENNIALS ARE THREE TIMES MORE LIKELY THAN BABY BOOMERS TO WATCH A VIDEO ON A MOBILE DEVICE.[50]

48   Maddy Osman, "18 Instagram Stats Every Marketer Should Know for 2018," sproutsocial, February 12, 2018, https://sproutsocial.com/insights/instagram-stats.

49   Mike Templeman, "17 Stats And Facts Every Marketer Should Know About Video Marketing," Forbes, September 6, 2017, https://www.forbes.com/sites/miketempleman/2017/09/06/17-stats-about-video-marketing/#56bff8de567f.

50   Jesica Mraz, "Why Millennials Love Online Video Content and Why You Should Focus On Them," YumYum Videos, March 31, 2016, http://go.yumyumvideos.com/blog/why-millennials-love-online-video-content-and-why-you-should-focus-on-them-and-make-an-explainer-video.

This means that while video is paramount to your connecting with Millennials in their buying journey, it's equally as important to test and make sure that the video displays properly on smartphones. Then, take it one step further. Make sure your videos are shareable.

> ## A WHOPPING 92 PERCENT OF VIEWERS WHO WATCH VIDEOS ON THEIR MOBILE PHONES SHARE THOSE VIDEOS WITH OTHERS.[51]

WHAT IT ALL MEANS

Remember, Millennials generally prefer texting over talking, mobile over desktop, and video over reading. In other words, Millennials are the exact opposite of their predecessors in terms of what they like and what they're most receptive to.

If you haven't created video on your website, LinkedIn profile, or Facebook business page about who you are, what you do, and how you do it, you're failing to optimize the ways in which you could connect with what will soon be your largest consumer market: Millennials. In order to compete, you must connect.

---

51   "Nearly All Mobile Video Viewers Are Mobile Video Sharers," eMarketer, January 7, 2013, https://www.emarketer.com/Article/Nearly-All- Mobile-Video-Viewers-Mobile-Video-Sharers/1009586.

Key Takeaways

☑ Video is the most effective way to deliver content to Millennials.

☑ Millennials connect with video because it's a simple way to digest information.

☑ Videos are expected to gain more viewership than any other content by 2019.

☑ Marketers like creating videos because they're inexpensive and easy to produce.

☑ Nearly all of the most popular social media sites offer a video feature, allowing marketers greater penetration into these sites' greatest users, Millennials.

☑ The majority of video is viewed on smartphones, which means testing your video on mobile devices is critical.

☑ If you want to compete for Millennial business, you must connect by creating video.

CHAPT

TER 8

MILLENNIALS, MONEY, AND INVESTING

"Regardless of the role of automated investment advisors, RIAs will, at minimum, need an online presence to keep up in a millennial-servicing market. This means online services, social media, and mobile apps. It also means an efficient technology solution to allow their clients to browse qualified investment opportunities, public or private, and securely subscribe through an intuitive application."

—Ryan Gunn, Wealth Forge

Millennials are about to become huge players in the

investment field. According to Forbes, Baby Boomers are about to pass an estimated $30 trillion in assets down to this segment of the population within the next few years, giving Millennials the largest control and the uppermost hand on the world's wealth.[52]

Of course, if you're an investment firm, you have one question echoing through your mind after hearing this: how do we participate in that generational transfer? However, be advised that Millennials' approach to investing is distinct to previous generations and they handle money and choose the people who they entrust with that money very differently too, which will have several ramifications on how assets are allocated in the next three, five, ten, twenty, and thirty years. That's why discovering exactly how to connect with them so that they feel confident enough to trust you with their funds is critical.

---

52   Daniel Scott, "Hey Millennials, You Need to Speak Up About Your Inheritance," *Forbes*, October 9, 2017, https://www.forbes.com/sites/danielscott1/2017/10/09/hey-millennials-you-need-to-speak-up-about-your-inheritance/#f925db458240.

GETTING INSIDE THE MILLENNIAL MIND

Millennials and Baby Boomers are as different as rotary phones and text messages, manual locks and Uber, and newspapers and podcasts.

And they're just as varied in their viewpoints of success and allocation of material wealth.

Whereas their parents, Baby Boomers, valued having job stability—scaling the corporate ladder and growing a comfortable retirement stash as measures of success—Millennials are all about building their own businesses, working hard for themselves, and reaping the fruits of their own labor. Many in this generation are likely to lean toward entrepreneurship and take greater financial risks than their parents did because they're confident that even if they lose some money, they can earn it back—all important facts firms should keep in the back of their minds as they approach this generation and brainstorm investment solutions.

Another thing to bear in mind is that Millennials are extremely wary of Wall Street after the Great Recession, after which many of them were forced to take on student loans because their parents couldn't afford to pay for their college tuitions.

So if they're not entirely warm to the idea of Wall Street, what do Millennials trust? And where do they see themselves putting the $30 trillion they'll one day inherit?

MILLENNIALS AND INVESTMENTS

Millennials are impassioned about helping the world, doing good, and serving a purpose. This common trait shared among them has given rise to something called impact investing and Millennials are all about it. Impact investing is when you intentionally put money in companies, funds, or organizations that offer you both a financial return but also contribute a certain amount of funds toward creating a positive social or environmental impact that helps improve communities.

Companies, brands, or firms who willingly offer this kind of investing are embedding themselves in a special niche and generating a competitive edge over competitors.

Interestingly, impact investing isn't just a phenomenon that's popular only here in the US. Based on a study conducted on six continents by Bank of the West and a global investing forum called Toniic, 79 percent of Millennials claimed to be impact investors, proving this ideology isn't limited to just the US population.[53]

This is a telling fact about Millennials, showing that they have definitive opinions and strong viewpoints about who they want to invest their money with and where they believe it should go.

Because this generation is so unique in their thoughts, mentalities, and tastes, they also require a unique approach when it comes to investments. According to a study, 57 percent of them don't trust advisors, believing that they're more in it for self-serving material purposes than for their clients' best interests. Also, 51 percent claim that they try to completely dodge situations in which someone tries to tell them what to do.[54] What they want is someone who wants to build a relationship with them and works to gain their trust.

---

53 "Millennials & Impact Investment," Toniic Institute, with support from Bank of the West, Family Wealth Advisors, May 2016, https://www.toniic.com/wp-content/uploads/2016/05/Millennials-Impact-Investment-May-2016.pdf.

54 "Millennials & Money: The Millennial Investor Becomes a Force," Accenture Consulting, 2017, https://www.accenture.com/t00010101T000000Z__w__/au-en/_acnmedia/PDF-68/Accenture-Millennials-and-Money-Millennial-Next-Era-Wealth-Management.pdf.

This proves that the traditional model of expecting this generation to work with advisors in the capacity that Baby Boomers and Gen Xers have previously is likely a grave mistake. If advisors truly want to stay relevant in the investment game, they'll have to work hard to build rapport with this generation and show good will to retain them as clients both currently and into the future.

WHAT THEY'RE LOOKING FOR TODAY

Millennials of today have varied thoughts when it comes to their investment and financial goals. About 59 percent of them want to learn about budgeting and cash flow, 10 percent are immediately targeting short-term goals and want someone to offer insight into helping them achieve those goals, and only four out of ten are keen on planning for retirement.[55]

Given this and their thoughts about the investment space and advisors in general, what's the wisest approach to navigating this young crowd of investors? How can investment firms best position themselves to reap the business of this generation both today and in the coming years?

A HYBRID APPROACH

Speedy. Affordable. Mobile. Quality. Customized. These are only a handful of terms that describe what Millennials value. However, many Baby Boomers and Gen Xers have decided to turn a blind eye or remain blissfully oblivious to these ideals that Millennials appreciate, hoping that these expectations somehow miraculously bypass the

---

55   Ibid.

investment space. But hoping for that would be hoping in vain because there's just no such luck.

> **Speedy. Affordable. Mobile. Quality. Customized. These are only a handful of terms that describe what Millennials value.**

Millennials expect these words to apply to the investment space as much as they do anywhere else. After all, they grew up accustomed to these buzzwords infiltrating every corner and industry of their worlds.

But how can investment firms achieve all that? The simple answer is technology. Millennials love digital and are extremely tech-savvy, as we know. In fact, they're the most digitally savvy generation of investors in history, according to Accenture's Wealth in the Digital Age Investor survey.[56]

But while digital can offer the speed, economy, quality, etc., that Millennials desire, it can't ever completely replace the value of a real, live, human advisor—especially when it comes to the more complicated investing scenarios. This means that firms will have to use a hybrid approach of digital technology and advisors to deliver an optimized solution tailored for Millennials.

In fact, already, nearly two-thirds of Millennials claim to use a hybrid model to serve their investment needs.[57] Let's look at the value each of these two unique components provide.

---

56   Ibid.

57   Ibid.

TECHNOLOGY AND ROBO-ADVISORS ON THE RISE

If you're in the investment space, you're privy to the fact that apps like Robinhood and Acorns are popping up, replacing investment advisors. And why wouldn't they be? Millennials have already grown accustomed to managing money electronically through mobile deposits and electronic transfers, so they're not wrong to gravitate toward such conveniences in the investment space too.

Millennials' fondness for digital has already generated revolutionary advances, most popularly in the form of robo-advisors that provide advice and online investment management with little to no human interaction. Cost-effective and efficient, robo-advisors are continuing to gain tremendous popularity. Globally recognized banks such as Bank of America, Vanguard, and Charles Schwab have already hopped in, swift to seize, hold, and adopt these capabilities.

Although robo-advisors may take over routine portfolio management responsibilities, that's not to say that Registered Investment Advisors (RIAs) should be afraid of becoming completely obliterated. In fact, it's more likely that they'll be found valuable in servicing larger investment accounts using their strengths in personal touch and understanding of client preferences as great advantages in that space.

However, technology and robo-advisors are anticipated to play a heavy role in the investment world both today and into the future. Here are several statistics to give you a sense of why technology shows no signs of fading from this space—what Millennials want versus what Gen Xers and Baby Boomers want.

→ 67% want computer-generated recommendations (robo) as a basic component

- → Gen Xers and Baby Boomers: 30%

- → 65% want gamification that will help them learn more about investing, and keep them more engaged with their portfolio

- → Gen Xers and Baby Boomers: 39%

- → 62% want a platform that incorporates social media and sentiment indices to assist in financial recommendations

- → Gen Xers and Baby Boomers: 30%

- → 66% want a self-directed investment portal with advisor access

- → Gen Xers and Baby Boomers: 25%

- → 63% want a mobile platform that connects directly to advisors

- → Gen Xers and Baby Boomers: 27%

- → 67% want software that enables tracking of transactions, payments, and other financial data in real time to provide better recommendations

- → Gen Xers and Baby Boomers: 30%[58]

Also, Millennials are a self-service, self-education generation. They appreciate the autonomy that technology affords them in making their own decisions and being able to execute transactions without

---

58   "Millennials & Money: The Millennial Investor Becomes a Force," Accenture Consulting.

dependency, if they so choose. And if that technology and opportunity to self-serve isn't made available to them, they won't hesitate to take their business someplace where it is offered.

Combine that with the fact that Millennials prove a loyal breed once they like something or someone, that could potentially mean that once they're gone, you won't see them again.

Unfortunately, many financial organizations have been agonizingly slow to respond, allowing several start-ups to claim this opportunity and deliver simpler, more affordable methods in the fashion Millennials desire through digital platforms that reduce or completely forgo the need for them to speak face-to-face with an advisor.

Already, platforms like SoFi and Wealthfront serve as a testament to the success of these tech-driven models.

THE VALUE OF A HUMAN TOUCH

No matter how tech savvy and digital-crazy Millennials may be, there's no arguing that there are simply certain things technology cannot replace, like empathy and human emotions. A marriage, the birth of child, investing in a new venture—these are all milestone events that require careful planning and clarity that only another human can help provide. And Millennials, despite their love for digital, aren't oblivious to the value of a live advisor. Many times, they even prefer the one-on-one interaction for situations like the ones listed above.

Only 11 percent exclusively use a robo-advisor, which means there's still a lot of untapped opportunity for a human to step in, cover the gaps, and add value.[59]

---

59   Ibid.

Also keep in mind that Millennials are just at the onset of their investment years. As they inherit more wealth, earn greater wages, and have more complex finances, they'll become increasingly reliant on human advisors. However, they'll probably still scour the Internet first before speaking with anyone.

As you'll recall from previous chapters, Millennials place a huge importance on building trust and relationships, and only a real person can build that level of intimacy and confidence.

But investment advisors would be wise to amp up their technology game in the areas of social media and online tools because research proves that Millennials desire advisors who are digitally connected and can help them learn.

As you aim to accommodate the needs of Millennials by offering a robust, hybrid model to serve them and gain their business and confidence, here are some additional tips that will help you remain a valuable player in their books.

GIVE THEM A SEAMLESS EXPERIENCE

By now, you know Millennials are all about convenience and simplicity. Anything that takes away from that experience causes them to grow impatient or agitated, forcing them to take matters into their own hands, often at your detriment. This could mean they give up faith in you or turn to another competitor that removes the hurdles and roadblocks for them.

No website?

A difficult process to get in touch with an advisor?

Any of these could spell danger and send Millennial investors scurrying in the other direction. That's why technology is an ideal solution for them. It's a must-have, not a wish-to-have. Technology delivers the autonomy, convenience, and flexibility this group desires, removing the speed humps and delays most human processes are known for.

A must-have for financial advisors is the ability to send your Millennial clients a username and password where they can log in and see what products they are invested in and watch videos of the firm, listen to podcasts, view performance, etc.

Allow Millennials to customize their experience—for example, apps, resources, and learning materials—and you'll definitely win them over. By offering more digitally, traditional wealth management firms can take advantage of this opportunity to deliver a greater benefit over non-traditional competitors who are already stealing the show.

PAY ATTENTION TO THE LADIES

Many Baby Boomer women weren't too involved with household investments or finances—those were considered responsibilities of men. In fact, only 28 percent claimed that investment-related decisions were their cup of tea. But with Millennials, that's changed. Today, 40 percent of Millennial women say that investments are for them.[60] Also, Millennial women are more likely to inject their own cash into investments than the average American woman.

Having said that, wealth advisors would be wise to shift their focus to these rising female investors because it's likely that many of them are already controlling the purse strings of their households.

Also, females have ambitious plans for their retirement, with 70 percent of them expressing more concern about having sufficient

---

60 Nina Duraiswami, "Millennial Women Make Their Own Financial Future," Seeking Alpha, June 9, 2017, https://seekingalpha.com/article/4080436-millennial-women-make-financial-future.

money at retirement age than about having good health. This is a drastic difference over their male counterparts, of which only 46 percent shared similar concerns.[61] Also, women believe they need more money to retire comfortably, which presents a good opportunity for wealth advisors to step in and have more conversations around this topic with Millennial females.

GIVE THEM KNOWLEDGE

Millennials enjoy learning because they're accustomed to finding information on a whim. And while many of them believe themselves to be good at managing finances, 59 percent of them still demonstrate a willingness and desire to learn more about budgeting and cashflow.[62]

Advisors who take time to extend this value by mentoring and offering insight, then supplementing their teachings with some form of digital training, could make good headway in attracting Millennial business, confidence, and loyalty.

PROVIDE CONVENIENCE AND QUALITY— THEY WON'T MIND PAYING FOR IT

Millennials, we know, appreciate freebies and are value-conscious. So advisors shouldn't be surprised to find Millennials probing for fee information more aggressively than Baby Boomers did.

---

61   Michael S. Fischer, "How Millennial Women, Men View Retirement Differently: Schwab," ThinkAdvisor, November 15, 2016, https://www.thinkadvisor.com/2016/11/15/how-millennial-women-men-view-retirement-different.

62   "Millennials & Money: The Millennial Investor Becomes a Force," Accenture Consulting.

But this doesn't mean that Millennials are necessarily stingy. Show them value, a quality product, or a rare convenience and they'll prop open their wallets faster than you'd expect.

However, be mindful of how you charge for your novelty, because unlike Baby Boomers, Millennials prefer flat fees over commission-based pay models, just because that's what they're most familiar with through the advents of Netflix and Uber. Firms who practice only a fee-based model would be wise to modify their fee systems for this generation.

> **Unlike Baby Boomers, Millennials prefer flat fees over commission-based pay models, just because that's what they're most familiar with through the advents of Netflix and Uber.**

WHERE MILLENNIALS INVEST

This group of investors favors commodities and options and they're also twice as likely to put money in ETF (exchange-traded funds) than their Baby Boomer parents.

PUBLIC VERSUS PRIVATE MARKETS

Although private markets are considered higher risk than public, technology and regulations have permitted them to be much more transparent with shareholders. And if there's one thing you should know about Millennials, it's that they appreciate transparency.

Public markets are also known to comprise of oil companies, large banks, and gas companies—all of which Millennials are known to be indifferent to or wary of, which is only in part the reason they're more likely to step toward private investments.

TIPS FOR SUCCESS WITH MILLENNIALS

Investment firms looking for a checklist of salient points to help them best serve the Millennial generation both now and into the future can keep these simple tips in mind:

➜ **CREATE TRUST AND BE TRANSPARENT:**
Foster relationships, customize your advice, and be crystal clear about fees. When hiring financial firms, it would be wise to select talent that can also put this advice into practice by being personable and knowing how to build trust.

➜ **BE A GREAT COMMUNICATOR:**
Everyone is different. Find out how your Millennial client likes to communicate (text, email, messaging via a digital investment content platform or the phone) and communicate with them in that manner. And when you are communicating, be an advisor not a dictator. Millennials appreciate insight but they still like to be the one controlling decisions that impact them.

➜ **USE DATA TO CUSTOMIZE RECOMMENDATIONS:**
Track clients' online activity to gather data about them and use this in conjunction with their personal preferences to send them customized investment ideas, alerts, and recommended products.

→ **EXPLORE TECHNOLOGY:**
Look for ways to leverage technology to make experiences simpler, more self-serving, and more convenient for Millennial users. Robo-advisors and digital investment content platforms and tools are just the start of the options available to explore.

Key Takeaways

☑ Millennials have a different approach to finances and investments than previous generations.

☑ They favor impact investing, or investing that offers financial returns but also creates a positive social impact.

☑ While technology and self-service drive them, Millennials also appreciate a human touch in the investment space, meaning a hybrid of tech and human would be the ideal mix for them.

☑ Millennials don't like encountering "friction" in their business dealings. They appreciate simplicity and convenience. If they find it inconvenient or complicated to do business with you, they'll do it with someone else.

☑ Follow these tips to create the best business relationship and experience for Millennial investors.

CHAP

TER 9

INVESTING IN THE IMPACT GENERATION

by Bill Davis, CIO of Stance Capital

Attaching labels to generations is a somewhat new, relatively informal practice that has no true science behind it. Nonetheless, it's fascinating that people who come of age at specific times in history are all similarly influenced and molded by the physical, social, economic, and political environments around them.

For instance, Tom Brokaw coined the term "The Greatest Generation" to label the cohort of Americans who grew up during the Great Depression, fought in World War II, and went on to make America a dominant economic power. And in his book, titled the same, he went on to characterize this generation's greatness as a selfless conviction that fighting in World War II was simply "the right thing to do."[63]

While it might be tough to top the "greatest generation," I believe Millennials will do just that. Historians will know Millennials as "The Impact Generation," and this chapter will demonstrate why this is their destiny.

THE IMPACT GENERATION DEFINED

There is a lot to unpack here, so let's start with the term "impact." In a broad sense, this means doing something that creates a positive outcome. As it relates to investing, things get a bit more complicated because "impact investing" is a defined term, but without a precise meaning.

But to offer some clarity, we'll go by the definition offered by Commmondfund Institute.[64] Impact investing is direct investments

---

63   Tom Brokaw, *The Greatest Generation* (New York: Random House, 1998).
64   Lauren Caplan et al., "From SRI to ESG: The Changing World of Responsible Investing," *Commonfund Institute*, September 2013, https://eric.ed.gov/?id= ED559300.

in specific companies, and even place-based projects, with the desired goal of effecting mission-related social or environmental change;

The terms socially responsible investing (SRI); environmental, social, governance Investing (ESG); and values-based investing are often used interchangeably within the broader category of impact investing, and represent a wide array of underlying value propositions and investment strategies. To avoid confusion between these approaches, we will default to the following definitions outlined by Commonfund Institute:

- **SRI** – a process that seeks to avoid investing in certain companies or industries through negative screening according to defined ethical guidelines

- **ESG** – integrating environmental, social, and governance factors with fundamental investment analysis to the extent they are material to investment performance in order to generate competitive returns

- **Values-based investing** – a newer concept that refers to an extension of ESG toward other values sets. These could include investing with a gender lens, or a focus on human rights, or faith, or something else entirely.

It's easy to see why the terms are confusing, as the intent of all approaches is the same: to align capital with values. This might mean extending micro-loans to create jobs in Ethiopia or tweaking a retirement account to make sure public equity holdings don't include weapons and tobacco companies. For the purposes of this chapter, when we refer to Millennials creating impact, we're really talking about all of the above, in both private and public investing.

Taking this a step further: Millennials will be the Impact Generation not just through their investments but also through their careers and as an expression of their personal brands. Fueled by technology and access to everything, this is the first generation that will favor experiences over material belongings, and will pursue social justice at least as vigorously as it pursues profit.

> **Millennials will be the Impact Generation not just through their investments but also through their careers and as an expression of their personal brands.**

I am reminded of an old expression that goes like this: "If you're not a liberal at twenty, you have no heart. If you're not a conservative at forty you have no brain." The point is that every generation of young people is full of dreams of making the world a better place. In this sense, today is no different than the 1960s or any other time of coming of age.

Except that Millennials' desire to make the world a better place today is less a youthful hope and more a stark necessity—taken alone, the physical, social, economic, and political challenges that surround Millennials are formidable. Taken together, there's really no alternative but to tackle the challenges head on.

THE NEED FOR ENVIRONMENTAL, SOCIETAL, AND ECONOMIC IMPROVEMENTS

Let's start with the environment. While previous generations wrestled with pollution, that's a low-level version of what the world faces today. Millennials have inherited the problems associated with climate risk, and there are many of them: coastal flooding, more violent storms, record-breaking heat each year, wild fires, drought, famine, lack of water, global dislocation, geo-political wars, disease, pandemics, and other such climate-related tragedies.

That alone might be enough, but let's consider societal challenges. Notwithstanding a strong economy, one in every six Americans is food insecure, and most are living paycheck to paycheck, while the income gap between the wealthiest and poorest Americans continues to widen. As *inequality.org* points out, "The rich don't just have more wealth than everyone else. The bulk of their wealth comes from different—and more lucrative—asset sources. America's top 1 percent, for instance, holds nearly half the national wealth invested in stocks and mutual funds. Most of the wealth of Americans in the bottom 90 percent comes from their principal residences, the asset category that took the biggest hit during the Great Recession. These Americans also hold almost three-quarters of America's debt."[65]

Speaking of debt, according to Jack Friedman at Forbes, in 2017, student debt in the US crossed the $1.3 trillion mark, making it the second-highest consumer debt category, behind only mortgage debt.[66] Graduates in their twenties now spend, on average, $350 per

---

65   "Wealth Inequality in the United States." *Inequality.org*, 29 May 2018, inequality. org/facts/wealth-inequality/.

66   Zack Friedman, "Student Loan Debt In 2017: A $1.3 Trillion Crisis," Forbes, February 21, 2017, https://www.forbes.com/sites/zackfriedman/2017/02/21/

month paying down student debt; and as Sarah Landrum, writer and founder of Punched Clocks, points out in Forbes, "There are many kinds of freedom, but very few of them are possible to achieve without financial dignity."[67]

The flip side of student debt is an educated workforce. Millennials represent the best-educated generation in US history, but with 80 million members, and a changing nature of jobs in America, unemployment and under-employment combined with heavy debt burden create significant financial challenges for this cohort.

According to Pew Research Center, Millennials are "the first in modern era to have higher levels of student loan debt, poverty, and unemployment, and lower levels of wealth and personal income than any other generation at the same stage of life."[68]

Beyond economics, Millennials are both racially and ethnically diverse, and are concerned about a wide variety of social justice areas including racial discrimination, women's health and reproductive issues, healthcare in general, and immigration. This perhaps explains a decidedly more liberal outlook than previous generations. In *The Generation Gap in American Politics*, Pew Research Center looks at political preferences of various generations through the lens of first-year job approval ratings of US presidents. Unsurprisingly, the single biggest approval gap belongs to Millennials. Obama had a 64 percent approval rating after one year in office. Trump is at 27 percent

student-loan-debt-statistics-2017/#f673dd15daba.

67   Sarah Landrum, "Millennials, Technology and The Challenge of Financial Literacy," Forbes, August 7, 2017, www.forbes.com/sites/sarahlandrum/ 2017/ 08/04/millennials-technology-and-the-challenge-of-financial-literacy/#4b8acc6128e6.

68   Bruce Drake, "6 New Findings about Millennials," Pew Research Center, March 7, 2014, www.pewresearch.org/fact-tank/2014/03/07/6-new-findings-about-millennials.

approval after his first year. In contrast, Boomers were at 50 percent for Obama and 44 percent for Trump.[69]

Hopefully the picture is becoming clearer. Millennials have a lot of challenges facing them, and even without much money (yet!), they are making their intentions known. Given the dysfunctional political climate in the United States, (and remember, it has been this way for over seventeen years, so basically it's the only political environment Millennials have ever known) young Americans have increasingly turned to corporations to drive the social changes they expect.

Let's examine their relationship with corporations, as this informs their approach to brand preferences, career decisions, and impact investing.

MILLENNIALS' TAKE ON THE RESPONSIBILITY OF CORPORATIONS

In a 2017 Cone Communications Research Study, the authors point out that Millennials expect companies to play a significant role in creating positive social change. Put another way, they expect the companies they work for and buy products and services from to not only have strong corporate social responsibility (CSR) practices, but also values that align with their own. Millennials reward companies that show effort and positive results, and they punish companies that are socially tone-deaf and insincere.[70]

---

69   "The Generation Gap in American Politics," http://www.pewresearch.org/, March 1, 2018, www.people-press.org/2018/03/01/the-generation-gap-in-american-politics.

70   "2017 Cone Communications CSR Study," http://www.conecomm.com/Research-Blog/2017-Csr-Study, May 17, 2017, www.conecomm.com/ research-blog/2017-csr-study.

Consider Under Armour for a moment. The CEO was recently ranked by 24/7 Wall Street as one of the worst CEOs in America.[71] To be sure, this ranking is driven by financials, not social issues, and given its stock has lost four to five of its value over the past three years, it's easy to see why the CEO is on the list (at number four). But a contributing factor was his endorsement of Donald Trump in 2016 and the resulting brand impact with its younger, more educated customers. Mismanaged social issues contributed to financial woes.

Another example: Papa John's. The founding CEO was forced to resign over poor performance, which he subsequently blamed on the impact of NFL players' anthem protest on pizza sales. Despite wide criticism of his comments, a neo-Nazi media outlet then endorsed Papa John's as the pizza company for the alt-right, which created still more problems. But despite mismanaging the NFL's political crisis, this company has been facing social headwinds for years. Millennials care about healthy food and thus disfavor pizza companies such as Papa John's. And further, the CEO had well documented worl views that align with far-right politics. Again, not something to be rewarded by Millennials.

While Papa John's, Under Armour, and others have been making bad social responsibility decisions, Patagonia took a different path and in December of 2017 strongly advocated against the Trump Administration's decision to scale back protection of several national monuments. They subsequently sued the Trump Administration. And were rewarded with increased sales from environmentally active (notably Millennial) consumers. Today, Patagonia's website has a section called Patagonia Action Works. Essentially it is a portal with

---

71 Douglas McIntyre and Jon Ogg, "20 Worst CEOs in America 2017," 24/7 Wall St, December 26, 2017, https://247wallst.Com/Special-Report/2017/12/26/Worst-Ceos-in-America-2017/2.

an interactive map that connects consumers to local grantees funded by Patagonia, tackling problems in areas such as biodiversity, climate, communities, land, and water. When you buy something from the website, the very last thing you see is a page showing that they are donating 1 percent of your sale to an environmentally focused organization in your local area.

Which clothing company do you think Millennials want to work for, buy products from, or invest in: Under Armour or Patagonia? The contrast isn't always this stark, but Millennials will do their homework to get to the truth, and then reward or punish brands. And then they'll use social media to spread the word. As you read this, it may seem as though I am making a political argument, but actually, I am talking about risk. Companies are people and people have values, so it's hard to keep values away from Corporate America. And when politics in America was mostly different shades of the same color, none of this really mattered. But when you combine divergent values with massive buying power, and the intent to link commerce with social justice, this poses significant risk to companies on the wrong side of this generation.

Authenticity matters. While most people view brands as an extension of themselves, younger Americans are willing to pay more for products and services from companies that earn their endorsement. And the cost to the companies is authenticity, as Cone's CSR study also points out: "Americans expect companies to stand up for issues far outside their operational footprints—from immigration to LGBTQ rights. Companies should determine if they can authentically stand up for social justice issues and be prepared to step into the spotlight."[72]

---

72   Ibid.

So what does this all have to do with investing? Everything—as Millennials will want their financial investments to reflect their core values. Before we dive into this topic lets first examine their wealth today.

> **Younger Americans are willing to pay more for products and services from companies that earn their endorsement.**

MILLENNIALS' WEALTH

As already noted, Millennials don't have much in the way of investable assets. When the youngest Millennials graduated from college in 2017, student debt averaged $37,000.[73] No wonder so many members of this generation are still living with their parents and renting as opposed to owning.

Interestingly, Millennials are often tagged as lazy with their money for paying more for products and services that line up with their values. It's a misleading label at best and fails to capture what is really going on, which is that Millennials are savers (but not necessarily investors), and for good reason. They've witnessed the Great Recession and have a mutually distrustful employment relationship with Corporate America. They've experienced downsizing and flat wages, and generally expect to be in a job for only a few years before moving on. Is this about the money? Sometimes, but it is often for culture or social justice reasons. The point is that between debt and

---

73   Zack Friedman, "Student Loan Debt In 2017: A $1.3 Trillion Crisis."

sometimes self-imposed job uncertainty, saving is more important than investing. More affluent Millennials tend to buy individual stocks of companies they endorse and respect, and more often than not these are tech stocks such as Apple, Netflix, and Amazon.

Interestingly, the generation that lived through the Great Depression and fought in World War II most closely represents Millennials in many ways. (The Great Depression vs. The Great Recession) and, (Nazi Germany and Imperial Japan vs. climate risk and geopolitical threats.) Just as their grandparents did before them, they will rise to these challenges without losing their core values, and as they acquire wealth, they will put this wealth to good use.

THE TRANSITION FROM SOCIALLY RESPONSIBLE INVESTING (SRI) TO ENVIRONMENTAL, SOCIAL, AND GOVERNANCE (ESG) INVESTING

Most of the wealth soon to be in motion to Millennials is currently guarded by (mostly Baby Boomer) financial advisors and firms that have a decidedly different world view and one informed by their own experiences. To Baby Boomers, socially responsible investing, which was the original name for what now falls under impact investing, is frivolous at best, and more likely deleterious to long-term investment returns. Under their way of thinking, if an investor cares about a specific cause—let's say lung cancer prevention—that investor should invest in such a way as to maximize returns, even if it means investing in tobacco companies. And then, with the profits, make charitable contributions to their favorite lung cancer prevention organization. Because the alternative, which in this example would be to construct a portfolio that excluded tobacco companies, creates risk of market underperformance.

In fairness, it's a reasonable argument for two reasons. The first is that assuming the return streams are better if tobacco companies are included, then the ability of the investor to create impact through charity is in fact greater—especially when you consider that $1 invested in the tobacco sector in 1900 would have yielded $6,280,237 by 2015, making tobacco the single highest-performing part of the economy to invest in over that 115-year history.[74]

The second reason advisors tend to dissuade clients from socially responsible investing is a bit subtler. If our hypothetical investor concerned about lung cancer decides to divest from a tobacco stock, another investor will come in and buy the stock, so the tobacco company isn't punished. And if the investor underperforms as a result, the big loser is the charity, as there is less money available to distribute to them.

For these reasons, the socially responsible investing movement—which got going in the 1970s in response to apartheid—never really went mainstream. There will always be investors who want negative exclusions of an industry or two from their portfolios, but advisors advocating that such an approach is a bad idea have outnumbered their investors. And advisors jobs were made easier because SRI strategies tended to underperform their benchmarks.

This said, SRI gave way to ESG in 2013 or so, and the easiest way to explain the difference is that SRI was about negative exclusions (tobacco, weapons, coal, etc.), whereas ESG looks at the

---

74 Elroy Dimson et al., "Credit Suisse Global Investment Returns Yearbook 2015," Credit Suisse, Febuary 1, 2015, https://psc.ky.gov/pscecf/2016-00370/ rateintervention%40ky.gov/03312017050856/Dimson_et_al_-_Credit_Suisse_- _2015_Investment_Returns_Yearbook.pdf.

economy as a whole and excludes companies from each sector that are poor stewards of the environment, badly governed, and detached from social justice issues. Because ESG is less about exclusion and more about inclusion of well-run companies, underperformance is no longer a major issue. Indeed, it is now possible to outperform conventional investment approaches, including index funds through ESG investing. As a result, assets are starting to flow into ESG strategies, as well as other values-based investment strategies and portfolio management firms that are rushing to bring new ESG products into the marketplace.

Don't get too hung up on the math, as I believe there is some double counting going on here, but according to US SIF 2016 annual report, of the $40 trillion of investment assets under professional management in the US, $8.72 trillion of these assets have incorporated ESG/SRI/values-based themes. Responsible investing is growing at 33 percent per year in the US. To be clear, this isn't all retail money.[75] Far from it as the number includes assets from public pensions, endowments, and faith-based organizations. In a recent report from McKinsey & Company the authors state, "More than one-quarter of assets under management globally are now being invested according to the premise that environmental, social, and governance (ESG) factors can materially affect a company's performance and market value."[76]

One way big institutional investors protect their investments is by working with corporations to ensure that management teams get focused

---

75   Meg Vorhees and Farzana Hoque, "2016 Annual Report: US SIF and US SIF Foundation,"US SIF, 2016, https://www.ussif.org/files/Publications/2016USSIFAn nualReport_online.pdf.

76   Sara Bernow, Bryce Klempner and Clarisse Magnin, "From 'Why' to 'Why Not': Sustainable Investing as the New Normal," McKinsey&Company, www. mckinsey.com/industries/private-equity-and-principal-investors/our-insights/ from-why-to-why-not-sustainable-investing-as-the-new-normal.

on ESG factors that represent material risk. These factors will vary by industry and some are common across all industries, such as pension fund status, management and board diversity, and executive compensation. We'd all agree that water usage isn't a big thing, for instance, for a bank. But it is a big thing in a beverage company or a utility. Not only do they use a lot of water, their businesses depend on water. Investors want them to mitigate this risk by being thoughtful stewards of water as an asset.

This emerging ecosystem has built-in feedback mechanisms. Investors push for progress and if they don't get it they vote their shares against the board and management. Public companies increasingly disclose annual corporate social responsibility reports, which then allow investors to compare and contrast multiple companies in the same industry groups in order to decide which are best managing ESG risks. This process applies to both equity and corporate bonds. The data is increasingly transparent, and all stakeholders in the ecosystem have access to it. Millennials are already stakeholders as well in that they are signaling the social behaviors they expect in return for their consumer loyalty.

There is one broken link in the ecosystem, however, and that is the financial advisor community. According to Cerulli Associates, as of the beginning of 2017, there were 310,504 financial advisors in the US, half of which plan to retire in the next ten years.[77] In general, these advisors formed the opinion many years ago that SRI = underperformance, and many haven't grasped the shift underway in which investors are increasingly looking to align capital with values

---

77   "Number of US Financial Advisors Fell for Fifth Straight Year –Report," Reuters, Febuary 11, 2015, www.reuters.com/article/wealth-cerulli-advisor-headcount/number-of-u-s-financial-advisors-fell-for-fifth-straight-year-report-idUSL1N-0VL23920150211.

and now have the tools to do so without sacrificing performance. Financial advisors need to get caught up, as most don't understand the difference between SRI and ESG, let alone more nuanced values sets, and are dismissive of the effort. But clients of all generations are starting to understand and ask for more sustainable investment options, and this is before Millennials enter the investment picture and change everything.

WHAT TODAY'S INVESTORS ARE LOOKING FOR

Big themes for today's investors are low-carbon strategies, as well as avoiding lightning rod issues such as AR15 manufacturers. For clients worried about the effects of climate change on their children and grandchildren, chances are they are trying to make changes in their lives to do their part. This might include swapping their SUV for an electric or hybrid vehicle or installing solar panels on their roof. They might have made the decision, maybe prompted by their Millennial or Gen Z kids, to stop buying throwaway plastic water bottles. If so, they also might be reusing grocery bags and filling them with more fruits and vegetables. You get the idea.

Even after doing all of this, let's say their family carbon footprint is roughly a hundred metric tons per year, which is actually twice the national average for a family of three.

Now let's say this same family has a million dollars invested in an S&P 500 index fund. It turns out that in this new age of data transparency we know a lot about every company in the S&P 500. We know the combined market cap is $21 trillion. We also know that the Scope 1 and 2 carbon emissions of the S&P 500 as a whole are 4,300 million tons per year.

To bring this math together, when someone invests a million dollars in an S&P 500 index fund, they own an additional 227 metric tons of carbon, each and every year. As today's investors begin to understand they have choices including lower carbon investment strategies, we will see a shift in this direction. But what about the Millennial investors just around the corner? Is there any reason to believe they won't demand low carbon investment options?

The better question might be: what are the chances today's advisors will hold onto tomorrow's clients?

MILLENNIALS AS INVESTORS OF THE FUTURE—AND THEIR IMPACT ON FINANCIAL ADVISORS

Sixty-six percent of children fire their parents' financial advisor after they inherit their parents' wealth, according to an *Investment News* survey completed last year.[78]

With that data as a benchmark, my answer to the earlier question would be somewhere between slim and none. I say this because the advisor community as a whole has struggled to understand and embrace this broad-based, multigenerational movement toward sustainability and impact creation. Or maybe they don't believe in climate risk. Or they are nearing retirement and can't be bothered. For an increasing number of Americans, and for most Millennials and Gen Zers, this is a fight for their lives and for those of their children's.

---

78   Liz Skinner, "The Great Wealth Transfer Is Coming, Putting Investors at Risk," Investment News, July 13, 2015, www.investmentnews.com/article/20150713/ FEATURE/150719999/the-great-wealth-transfer-is-coming-putting-advisors-at-risk.

Unlike their grandfathers who fought in WWII with guns and bullets, Millennials are armed with technology, social media, and the desire to self-educate. They understand how all the pieces come together. They have built-in bullshit detectors. They realize that corporations are critical to both the fight for social justice and a healthy planet. And even without much money, they are forcing corporations to change for the better—at least the ones looking to access the bulk of an eighty-million-member consumer marketplace.

Does anyone actually think that Millennials will own investment funds that hold companies they detest? There are plenty of Baby Boomers who detest Fox News and probably just as many who feel the same way about CNN. But how many will go through the effort to figure out which index or mutual fund owns the parent company, sell the fund, and then research alternatives? And how many of today's advisors will show them the path? Very few, but no matter, as Millennials can find that path themselves quite easily.

The financial services winners in the largest generational wealth transfer ever will be the brave few that get out in front of this process. Just because clients haven't asked about sustainability doesn't mean they don't care about it. There are good products in the marketplace already and advisors need to educate themselves so they are no longer the sand in the machine, but rather the lubricant needed to demand quality ESG products on their investment platforms, and then get these products in front of families. And by the way, not all of this need be equity products. There are a wide number of private investment products available in everything from biodegradable plastics to solar energy deployments. The good news is that Millennials will pay more for solutions that provide a public benefit, but it will be hard to fool them if the approach isn't authentic.

I'll end where we started. We already have the "greatest" generation. Millennials will be known as the "impact" generation and will accomplish at least as much as their predecessors dealing with modern-day problems at least as thorny. For financial services firms and advisors who authentically embrace the ways in which Millennials look at the world and show the willingness to invest in products and services that meet their needs, it will be both prosperous and transformative.

Key Takeaways

☑ Millennials will be known as the Impact Generation for investing in companies that offer them both financial gain and aim to make a positive impact on the world, socially and/or economically.

☑ Millennials believe that corporations have a social responsibility to promote change in the world.

☑ Dollars of this generation will continue to be given to businesses and brands that serve important roles in making a difference to society.

☑ Investment advisors should embrace how Millennials look at the world and help them invest in solutions that meet their visions.

CONCL

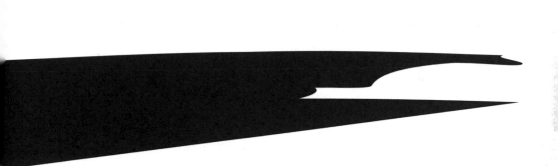

One day, I was explaining the benefits of the Stage Investor Network platform to an investment manager. After some contemplation, he asked me, "What happens if nothing happens for us on your platform, say, 365 days from now?"

"Awesome," I told him. "Day one you were introduced to three thousand investors who had never before heard of you nor you of them. What about day 366? Or day 730?"

My point was this: fundraising isn't linear. If you stick with it, there's always opportunity lurking around the corner. But that's a big if. You have to give consumers a reason to care about you. You have to provide insight. You have to be able to be found, and once you're found, you have to provide value.

That you've made it this far in the book makes it clear that you're here because you want to experience future successes. And I'm confident there's opportunity out there for you, because, from an investment standpoint, every professional investor in the US and abroad wants to explore new and interesting investment ideas. People want to learn about your strategy. All you have to do is keep everything you've learned at the forefront of your mind, apply it, be persistent, and you'll see results.

The same goes for any business owner. Application is key. Mindset is key.

You've been introduced to a lot of information. Some components and concepts may have been more foreign to you than others, so I suspect you'll need some time to soak it all in before you ponder next steps.

The bottom line is this: we live in a Content Economy, or an era in which digital content has quite literally changed the way people buy with Millennials leading the change. This generation is due to control the majority of the world's wealth in just a few short years.

If you desire to preserve your business from the volatility of change and would like to see it grow and thrive, you should understand and adapt to the nuances of the Content Economy, and keep Millennials at the forefront of your sales strategies. Sell to your consumers differently. Experiment with new tactics, like blogs, videos, podcasts, and social media to cater to this generation. These are the avenues that will help your business relate to buyers. These are the channels of the Content Economy. These are what buyers use to buy from everyone.

Those in the investment space, too, must evolve in tune to this Content Economy. Creating video is paramount to your success in this space. It's the best way to offer meaningful, easy-to-digest content. The absence of this evolution in financial firms is already proving challenging for buyers (predominantly Millennials) but also for investment managers (predominantly Baby Boomers and Gen Xers) who aren't able to effectively connect and develop a fruitful relationship with each other.

The differences in these three generations are drastic. The environments they were raised in, the world around them as they were coming of age and the existence, or lack thereof, of technological facets has influenced their behaviors, cultivating them into distinct segments of the population.

Content also gives you free feedback. Without content, you have no user engagement. You can't get into the minds of your buyers if you're not able to engage with them. And without user engagement, you have no data or analytics. Data is critical because it's what guides you to improve upon your existing business model. Without it, you won't know how to modify your business to the needs of today's day and age and to your primary target audience—the Millennials.

Before you begin adapting to the Content Economy and your new buyers, you must rewire your mindset first. The Content Economy can be a painful pill to swallow for Baby Boomers and Gen Xers because it involves significant change from tactics you're accustomed to and have been accustomed to for many years now. But unless your mind is prepped and ready, you cannot start taking action.

Once you've rewired your mindset, you have to show up, jump in, and get started. That sounds easier than it actually is because of an innate human tendency called akrasia, which promotes procrastination within the best of us. Be aware and cognizant of akrasia, and learn how to actively beat it. Because there's no place for procrastination in the Content Economy.

Investment firms must remember that Millennials invest using their hearts. They are loyal to brands that are in sync with their beliefs, are transparent, and are genuine. And they desire both financial gains and positive social and economic impacts to come about as a result of those investments. Investment firms should consider how to get in on these types of initiatives and support Millennials in their impact investment goals.

Apart from that there's something else to consider: As they step into positions of greater authority and power, Millennials will, without a doubt, modify their business strategies to sell to people of their generation exactly as they wish to be sold to, which puts the rest of us on a timed collision course. Because when Millennials are in power, we're going to be stepping onto a completely new playing field, and those who don't play by their rules won't get to play at all.

Finally, I applaud you for taking time to learn what's ahead. Educating yourself is an important feat in the Content Economy— and a surefire way to ensure you have the ammunition to forge ahead.

I wish you all the best. I wish you success in developing a growth mindset. I wish you an abundance of motivation and confidence as you embark on getting started. I wish you much patience and perseverance as you begin your journey on creating great content that will leave your buyers yearning to be a part of your success story forever. I wish you tons of prosperity and boatloads of success in all your endeavors. May adapting to the Content Economy introduce you to just the beginning of your successes.

With best wishes and warmest regards,
Gui Costin

APPE

NDIX

ADDITIONAL
RESOURCES AND
SUPPORTING
REFERENCES

Reference books that reiterate the points made in this book and will help you through the transition in effectively marketing to how Millennials buy today:

Exponential Organizations, **by Salim Ismail with Michael S. Malone and Yuri Van Geest**

Goes into detail about how companies nowadays perform and grow at an optimal level because they leverage technology—and how you can do the same.

The Platform Revolution, **by Geoffrey Parker, Marshall Van Alstyne, and Sangeet Paul Choudary**

Talks about the concept and significance of platforms and how to effectively build a platform business if you're a newbie.

Platform Scale, **by Sangeet Paul Choudary**

Unveils the growth, design, and strategy behind creating a successful platform.

Modern Monopolies, **by Alex Moazed and Nicholas L. Johnson**

Another book about platforms, but it starts at a rudimentary level, explaining the start of the platform era, what it means for businesses and how those businesses can adapt in this era.

The One Thing, **by Gary W. Keller and Jay Papasan**

Helps you learn the value of focusing your attention on a single goal to see that aspect of your life expand and grow in incredible ways.

The Untethered Soul: The Journey Beyond Yourself, **by Michael Singer**

Talks about learning who you are and defining your identity by tapping into your consciousness and by observing.

The Surrender Experiment, **by Michael Singer**
The inspirational story of a man who stopped trying to control life and instead let it guide him.

80/20 Sales and Marketing, **by Perry Marshall**
A book that shows you just how much money you're losing out on—and how to reclaim it.

The War of Art, **by Steven Pressfield**
Walks you through exactly how to defeat resistance and overcome the fears that prevent you from reaching your maximum abilities.

Insanely Simple: The Obsession That Drives Apple's Success, **by Ken Segall**
Discusses how simplicity is at the core root of everything Apple embodies—and how simplicity and clarity rule in today's world.

The Four: The Hidden DNA of Amazon, Apple, Facebook, and Google, **by Scott Galloway**
A discussion about how four major companies have come to infiltrate our lives so completely and thoroughly that we can't live without them—and how you can apply their secrets to your business.

Mindset: The New Psychology of Success, **by Carol Dweck**
A powerful read that talks about how your thinking shapes every aspect of your life—and directly leads to the outcomes you experience.

THE CENTER FOR GENERATIONAL KINETICS

HIGHLIGHTED NATIONAL RESEARCH STUDY FINDINGS

PREPARED FOR

STAGE INVESTOR NETWORK

CONFIDENTIAL

NATIONAL STUDY GOALS

○ **Reveal** the attitudes, trends, and perceptions behind Millennial purchase preferences.

○ **Uncover** the primary drivers and motivational factors involved in Millennials accessing online information and **making online purchase** decisions as well as their preferences for different types of online content.

○ **Capitalize** on the research findings to position Dakota Funds and it's leadership as the research-based thought leader in the industry.

2/39

ABOUT THE CENTER FOR GENERATIONAL KINETICS

- #1 Generational research, consulting, and speaking firm

- Over 180 clients per year, spanning every major industry

- Separating myth from truth when it comes to Gen Z, Millennials, and generations as employees, customers, and trendsetters

- The Center's work has been featured on hundreds of media outlets from *60 Minutes* to *The New York Times*

METHODOLOGY

- Custom 27-question survey designed collaboratively by Dakota Funds and The Center for Generational Kinetics

- Study was administered to 1,011 U.S. respondents ages 22-40 who have made an online purchase in the past 3 months. The sample was weighted to current U.S. Census data for age, region, and gender.

- Survey was conducted online from April 16, 2018 to April 19, 2018

- Figures are statistically significant at the 95% confidence level. Margin of error is +/-3.1 percentage points

- Please note that "By Total" in any graph represents the sample as a whole

- All individuals mentioned in this study still fall under the defined screening criteria - Millennials who have purchased anything online in the past 3 months

SAMPLE OVERVIEW

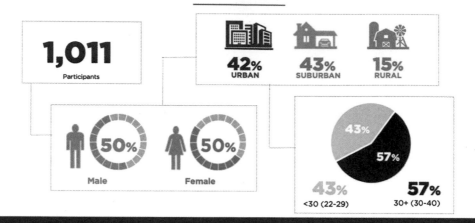

1,011
Participants

42% URBAN
43% SUBURBAN
15% RURAL

50% Male
50% Female

43%
57%

43%
<30 (22-29)

57%
30+ (30-40)

STUDY OVERVIEW

- Millennial Purchase Preferences
- Accessing Online Information
- Importance of Online Content in Making Decisions
- Millennials Preferred Type of Online Content

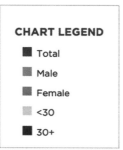

CHART LEGEND
- Total
- Male
- Female
- <30
- 30+

Most Millennials prefer a mix of in-person and online purchasing

Men prefer to buy more items in-person, while women are more likely to prefer an even split or a majority of purchases online.

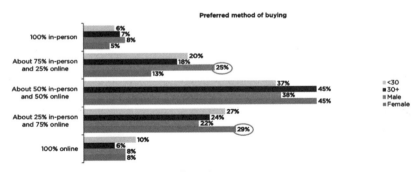

Preferred method of buying

100% in-person	6% / 7% / 8% / 5%	
About 75% in-person and 25% online	20% / 18% / 25% / 13%	
About 50% in-person and 50% online	37% / 45% / 38% / 45%	
About 25% in-person and 75% online	27% / 24% / 22% / 29%	
100% online	10% / 6% / 8% / 8%	

Legend: <30, 30+, Male, Female

Q10. Do you prefer to buy products online or in-person? Please select one.

But, over 2/3 of Millennial shoppers would ideally like an important purchase experience to happen online

Those under 30 and women are more likely to prefer a fully online purchase experience.

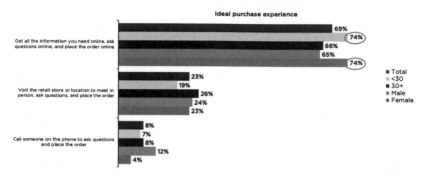

Ideal purchase experience

Get all the information you need online, ask questions online, and place the order online
- 69%
- 74%
- 66%
- 65%
- 74%

Visit the retail store or location to meet in person, ask questions, and place the order
- 23%
- 19%
- 26%
- 24%
- 23%

Call someone on the phone to ask questions and place the order
- 8%
- 7%
- 8%
- 12%
- 4%

- Total
- <30
- 30+
- Male
- Female

Q7. When you are considering making an important purchase, what is your ideal purchase experience? Please select one.

Over the last year, almost 2/3 of Millennials have increased their number of online purchases

Millennials making between $75K-$99K have found themselves making more purchases online over the last year compared to any other income group.

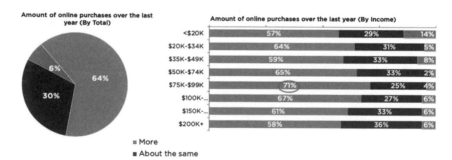

Amount of online purchases over the last year (By Total)
- 6%
- 64%
- 30%

Amount of online purchases over the last year (By Income)

Income	More	About the same	
<$20K	57%	29%	14%
$20K-$34K	64%	31%	5%
$35K-$49K	59%	33%	8%
$50K-$74K	65%	33%	2%
$75K-$99K	71%	25%	4%
$100K-...	67%	27%	6%
$150K-...	61%	33%	6%
$200K+	58%	36%	6%

- More
- About the same

Q11. Over the last year, have you found yourself making more purchases online than before, less, or the same as before? Please select one.

Over half of Millennials have decided against a purchase that made them pick up the phone or meet in person

In fact, nearly half of Millennial shoppers say they feel annoyed when a purchase requires a call or visit. Women are more likely to feel this way than men.

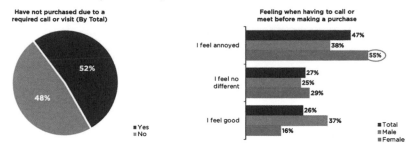

Have not purchased due to a required call or visit (By Total)

52%

48%

■ Yes
■ No

Feeling when having to call or meet before making a purchase

I feel annoyed — 47% / 38% / 55%

I feel no different — 27% / 25% / 29%

I feel good — 26% / 37% / 16%

■ Total
■ Male
■ Female

Q8. Have you ever not bought something because the purchase required you to make a phone call or visit with someone in person?

Q9. How do you feel when you have to make a phone call or meet with someone in person in order to make a purchase? Please select one

ACCESSING ONLINE INFORMATION

Millennials feel frustrated if they can't access the information they need online to make a purchase

Women are particularly frustrated when purchase information is not offered online, while men are more likely to feel fine or indifferent about this.

Feeling if a company does not offer all the information needed to make a purchase

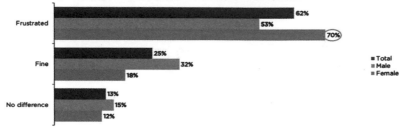

Q12. If a company does not offer all the information you need online in order to make a purchase, how do you feel? Please select one.

Companies without adequate online product information appear out-of-date and suspicious to Millennials

Women are much more likely then men to say that a company appears out-of-date when online information is lacking, while interestingly, men are more likely to not see this as such a negative.

Appearance of a company when they don't have adequate information online

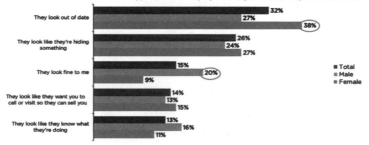

Q13. How does a company, brand, product, or service appear to you when they don't have all the information online that you need in order to make a confident purchase? Please select one.

Over half of Millennial consumers will lose trust in a company with limited online product information

Women are much more likely than men to lose trust as a result of limited product information.

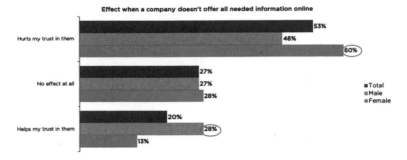

Effect when a company doesn't offer all needed information online

Hurts my trust in them	Total	53%
	Male	46%
	Female	60%
No effect at all	Total	27%
	Male	27%
	Female	28%
Helps my trust in them	Total	20%
	Male	28%
	Female	13%

■ Total
■ Male
■ Female

Q14. When a company does not offer all the information you need in order to make a buying decision online, how does that affect your trust in them? Please select one.

The majority of Millennials access online content to inform a buying decision on a weekly basis

31% of Millennial shoppers access online content at least once per day.

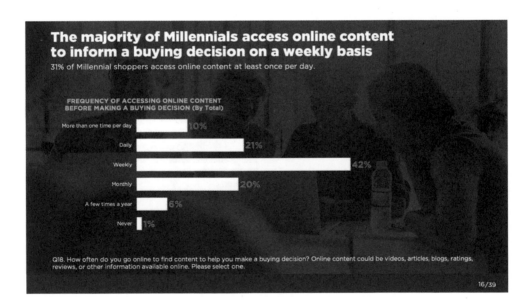

FREQUENCY OF ACCESSING ONLINE CONTENT BEFORE MAKING A BUYING DECISION (By Total)

More than one time per day	10%
Daily	21%
Weekly	42%
Monthly	20%
A few times a year	6%
Never	1%

Q18. How often do you go online to find content to help you make a buying decision? Online content could be videos, articles, blogs, ratings, reviews, or other information available online. Please select one.

More than half of Millennials are <u>very likely</u> to read ratings and reviews before making an online purchase

In fact, 82% of Millennial shoppers are likely or very likely to read ratings and reviews before purchasing online. Women are even more likely to do this than men.

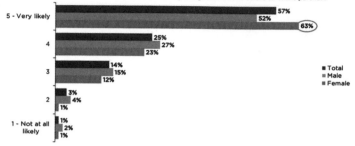

Likelihood of reading ratings and reviews before an online purchase

	Total	Male	Female
5 - Very likely	57%	52%	63%
4	25%	27%	23%
3	14%	15%	12%
2	3%	4%	1%
1 - Not at all likely	1%	2%	1%

Q16. How likely are you to read ratings or reviews before purchasing a product online? 1 = Not at all likely; 5 = Very likely

62% of Millennials spend 30 minutes or less researching an important product online before buying

However, 37% of Millennials will spend more than 30 minutes and 18% of these will spend more than an hour researching a product online before buying.

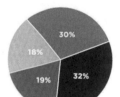

- 30%
- 18%
- 19%
- 32%

■ Less than 15 minutes
■ 16-30 minutes
■ 31-60 minutes
■ More than an hour

Time spent researching online before an important purchase (By Total)

None	1%
1-5 minutes	4%
6-10 minutes	11%
11-15 minutes	15%
16-20 minutes	14%
21-30 minutes	18%
31-40 minutes	9%
41-50 minutes	4%
51-60 minutes	6%
More than an...	18%

Q19. How much time do you spend researching an important product or service online before you buy? Please select one.

Millennials use smartphones and laptops the most for accessing online content before making a purchase

Women are much more likely than men to access online content using a smartphone. Men however, are almost equally as likely to use either a smartphone or laptop.

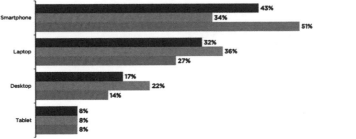

Preferred device for accessing online content about making a purchase

Device	Total	Male	Female
Smartphone	43%	34%	51%
Laptop	32%	36%	27%
Desktop	17%	22%	14%
Tablet	8%	8%	8%

■ Total
■ Male
■ Female

Q20. On what device are you most likely to access online content when you are looking up information about making a purchase? Please select one.

IMPORTANCE OF ONLINE CONTENT IN MAKING DECISIONS

Access to online content is vital to Millennials when making an important purchase

In fact, 2/3 of all Millennials feel that online content is important or very important when making an important purchase.

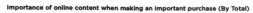

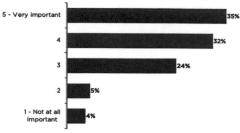

Importance of online content when making an important purchase (By Total)

- 5 - Very important: 35%
- 4: 32%
- 3: 24%
- 2: 5%
- 1 - Not at all important: 4%

Q1. How important is online content (informative videos, articles, blogs, information, etc.) to you when you have to make an important purchase? 1 = Not at all important; 5 = Very important

BIG money is lost from lack of online product information

<u>In the past month,</u> over half of Millennial shoppers decided to **not** carry through with a purchase due to a lack of online product information.

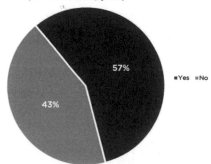

Decided not to purchase due to lack of online product information (By Total)

57%
43%

■Yes ■No

Q2. In the past month, have you decided to <u>not</u> make a purchase because you couldn't find the information you needed about the product or service online?

Online content can absolutely change a Millennial's purchase decision

The higher the income, the more likely that online content will influence Millennial consumers to make a different purchase decision than was originally intended.

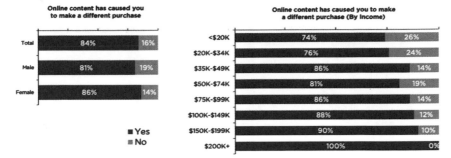

Online content has caused you to make a different purchase

	Yes	No
Total	84%	16%
Male	81%	19%
Female	86%	14%

Online content has caused you to make a different purchase (By Income)

	Yes	No
<$20K	74%	26%
$20K-$34K	76%	24%
$35K-$49K	86%	14%
$50K-$74K	81%	19%
$75K-$99K	86%	14%
$100K-$149K	88%	12%
$150K-$199K	90%	10%
$200K+	100%	0%

■ Yes
■ No

Q3. Has online content ever caused you to make a different purchase than the one you thought you would make?

Expensive or not, companies must have good online content that's easily available before Millennial shoppers will buy their products

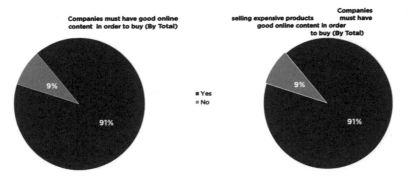

Companies must have good online content in order to buy (By Total)
9%
91%

Companies selling expensive products must have good online content in order to buy (By Total)
9%
91%

■ Yes
= No

Q4. Do you think companies must have good online content easily available about their product or service before you would make the decision to buy?

Q5. Do you think companies offering expensive products or services must have good online content easily available before you would make the decision to buy?

Companies with readily available online content are dramatically more likely to get Millennials' business

Also, for those Millennials making less than $200K, higher the income means increasing preference for a company that has readily available online content.

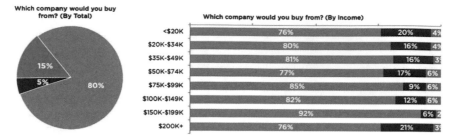

Which company would you buy from? (By Total)

- 15%
- 5%
- 80%

Which company would you buy from? (By Income)

Income	Company with online content	Company with no online content	Either one
<$20K	76%	20%	4%
$20K-$34K	80%	16%	4%
$35K-$49K	81%	16%	3%
$50K-$74K	77%	17%	6%
$75K-$99K	85%	9%	6%
$100K-$149K	82%	12%	6%
$150K-$199K	92%	6%	2
$200K+	76%	21%	3

- ▪ Company with online content
- ▪ Company with no online content
- ▪ Either one

Q6. If two companies were offering the same product or service but one company had readily available content online about their offerings and the other did not, which one would you buy from? Please select one.

Online content is becoming increasingly important for Millennials when making important purchases

Over the last year, 56% of Millennials relied on online content for important purchases more often than previously. This is especially true for Millennials making between $75K-$99K.

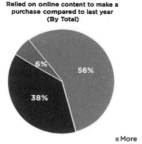

Relied on online content to make a purchase compared to last year (By Total)

- 6%
- 56%
- 38%

Relied on online content to make a purchase compared to last year (By Income)

Income	More	About the same	
<$20K	41%	44%	15%
$20K-$34K	50%	45%	5%
$35K-$49K	59%	36%	5%
$50K-$74K	55%	40%	5%
$75K-$99K	63%	31%	6%
$100K-...	59%	37%	4%
$150K-...	59%	37%	4%
$200K+	61%	33%	6%

- ▪ More
- ▪ About the same

Q17. Over the last year, have you relied on online content more, less, or about the same when it comes to making important purchases? Please select one.

The more important the purchase, the more Millennials access online content

This is especially true for women and older Millennials. Men, however, are more likely to say they access *less* online content when making an important purchase.

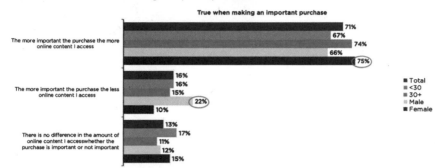

True when making an important purchase

The more important the purchase the more online content I access
- 71%
- 67%
- 74%
- 66%
- 75%

The more important the purchase the less online content I access
- 16%
- 16%
- 15%
- 22%
- 10%

There is no difference in the amount of online content I access whether the purchase is important or not important
- 13%
- 17%
- 11%
- 12%
- 15%

- Total
- <30
- 30+
- Male
- Female

Q15. When making an important purchase which of the following is true for you? Please select one.

Brands **must** have easily available online content in order for Millennials to make an important purchase

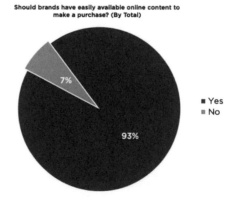

Should brands have easily available online content to make a purchase? (By Total)

- 7%
- 93%

- Yes
- No

Q21. Do you think brands, products, or services must have easily available online content about their offerings for you to make an important purchase?

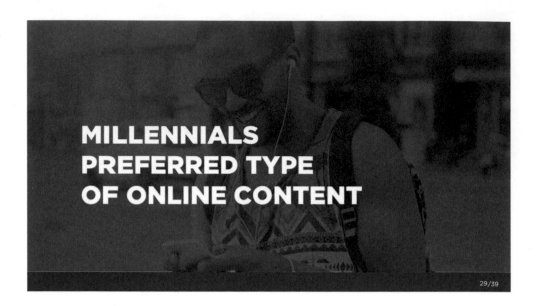

Millennials want to hear from real customers when making important purchase decisions

Over half of Millennials and 2/3 of women consider ratings or reviews from actual customers as influential in helping them make an important purchase decision.

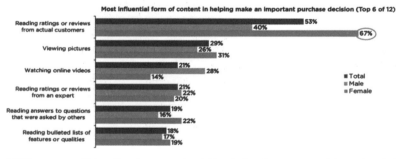

Most influential form of content in helping make an important purchase decision (Top 6 of 12)

Content	Total	Male	Female
Reading ratings or reviews from actual customers	53%	40%	67%
Viewing pictures	29%	26%	31%
Watching online videos	21%	28%	14%
Reading ratings or reviews from an expert	21%	22%	20%
Reading answers to questions that were asked by others	19%	16%	22%
Reading bulleted lists of features or qualities	18%	17%	19%

Q22. When you are considering making an important purchase decision, what form of content would you find most influential in helping you to make a decision? Please select your top two.

Millennial buyers find ratings, reviews, and pictures to be the most valuable for first time purchases

Women are much more likely than men to read ratings and reviews from actual customers and look at pictures when considering a new product.

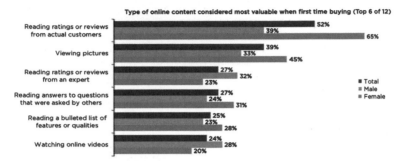

Type of online content considered most valuable when first time buying (Top 6 of 12)

Reading ratings or reviews from actual customers: Total 52%, Male 39%, Female 65%

Viewing pictures: Total 39%, Male 33%, Female 45%

Reading ratings or reviews from an expert: Total 27%, Male 32%, Female 23%

Reading answers to questions that were asked by others: Total 27%, Male 24%, Female 31%

Reading a bulleted list of features or qualities: Total 25%, Male 23%, Female 28%

Watching online videos: Total 24%, Male 28%, Female 20%

Q24. When you are considering buying a product or service for the first time, which of the following types of online content would you find the most valuable? Please select your top three.

Millennials are also most likely to share product content using ratings, reviews, and pictures

Women are much more likely to use ratings or reviews and pictures to share content, while men are much more likely to share content through online videos.

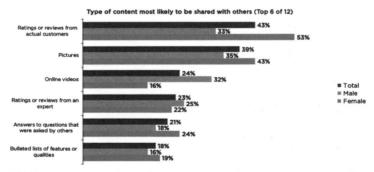

Type of content most likely to be shared with others (Top 6 of 12)

Ratings or reviews from actual customers: Total 43%, Male 33%, Female 53%

Pictures: Total 39%, Male 35%, Female 43%

Online videos: Total 24%, Male 32%, Female 16%

Ratings or reviews from an expert: Total 23%, Male 25%, Female 22%

Answers to questions that were asked by others: Total 21%, Male 18%, Female 24%

Bulleted lists of features or qualities: Total 18%, Male 16%, Female 19%

Q23. Which of the following types of content about a product or service are you most likely to share with others? Please select your top three.

FAQ and customer testimonial videos are the most influential to Millennial buying decisions

Women are much more influenced by FAQ and customer generated videos compared to men.

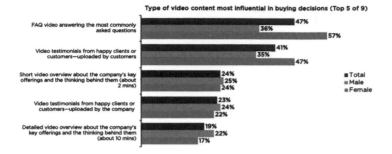

Type of video content most influential in buying decisions (Top 5 of 9)

FAQ video answering the most commonly asked questions
- 47%
- 36%
- 57%

Video testimonials from happy clients or customers—uploaded by customers
- 41%
- 35%
- 47%

Short video overview about the company's key offerings and the thinking behind them (about 2 mins)
- 24%
- 25%
- 24%

Video testimonials from happy clients or customers—uploaded by the company
- 23%
- 24%
- 22%

Detailed video overview about the company's key offerings and the thinking behind them (about 10 mins)
- 19%
- 22%
- 17%

■ Total
■ Male
■ Female

Q25. What type of video content would you find most influential in your buying decision? Please select your top three.

Bulleted text and visuals to illustrate key ideas are the most important to Millennials when reading an article

Women rate each of the top 5 article features as more important then men.

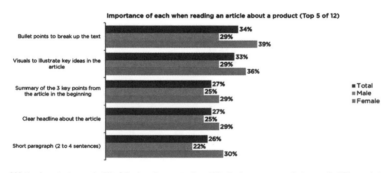

Importance of each when reading an article about a product (Top 5 of 12)

Bullet points to break up the text
- 34%
- 29%
- 39%

Visuals to illustrate key ideas in the article
- 33%
- 29%
- 36%

Summary of the 3 key points from the article in the beginning
- 27%
- 25%
- 29%

Clear headline about the article
- 27%
- 25%
- 29%

Short paragraph (2 to 4 sentences)
- 26%
- 22%
- 30%

■ Total
■ Male
■ Female

Q26. How important are each of the following when you read an article about a company, product, or service? Please select your top three.

Millennials are split on their preferences for a one stop online experience

More than half of Millennials still prefer to visit multiple different websites to inform their purchase decisions.

Preferred online experience when making a buying decision

Total	53%	47%
Male	57%	43%
Female	50%	50%

■ Visiting multiple different websites to find the information that you need
■ One website that already has videos, blogs, articles, and more in one place

Q27. When you are searching for content to make a buying decision, which of these online experiences do you prefer?

CONCLUSION

Millennials increasingly make purchases online and rely heavily on online content when researching purchases and making buying decisions. They highly value authenticity, trusting and valuing user generated content more than any other type of content.

IDEAS TO BUILD ON YOUR THOUGHT LEADER POSITION:

Based on what we found in your national study, this is what we believe will amplify your Defensible Difference~:

The Center's Core PR and Thought Leadership Solution:

- Take-Action White Paper or E-book fully branded to Dakota Funds (8 to 10 pages)

- Influencer Infographic with the 7 to 10 most powerful findings, fully branded

- Thought Leader Webinar (up to 60 minutes, recorded for ongoing use by Dakota Funds)

- Optional media expertise directly from Jason Dorsey

All thought leadership deliverables will be approved by Dakota Funds and will match your brand standards and positioning. Dakota Funds will own all of the deliverables

This completes the analysis of the findings from the Dakota Network national study. We are excited to work with you on your next study!

Gui Costin
Founder
e: gui@dakota.network
t: +1 (610) 764-0539

Dakota Network
925 Lancaster Avenue, Suite 220
Bryn Mawr, PA 19010

GLOS

SARY

Baby Boomers

A segment of the worldwide population that came about shortly after the end of World War II and is born approximately between the period of 1946-1964.

Buyer

A synonym for "due diligence analyst," a buyer is responsible for investing in strategies on behalf of an entity, for example, a mutual fund or Multi-Family Office. The buyer's job is to learn an in-depth amount about available strategies, analyze their risks, and compile information for an investment committee presentation where the strategy can be presented for buy-in to key decision makers.

Content Economy

An economy in which the presence of powerful, credible, authentic content, which replaces face-to-face communications, influences consumers' decisions about whether to buy and what to buy.

Due diligence analyst

see "Buyer."

Generation X

The generation after Baby Boomers, typically known as the "Latchkey Generation," born approximately between 1965–1980.

Investment manager

Someone who works on behalf of clients to invest their funds in portfolios of securities based on parameters set by clients. The investment manager may be responsible for buying and selling securities, monitoring portfolios, and fulfilling other tasks relevant to portfolio management.

Millennials

Also known as Generation Y, they are born roughly between 1981–1995.